THE PRAGMATIC CAT MAN

Kaylen Fletcher

Sparkmeister Productions

To some awesome people...

Thank you to my beautiful wife Ali who I'd be lost without and who helped me find an enriched life in a place I would never have thought of looking.

To my wonderful Bronagh, friend and editor who constantly goes above and beyond you have my deepest appreciation. I'm really not sure the world is ready for the sense of humour we produce together. Any gags that fall flat or cause offence I am going to blame on you.

Lastly a truly massive thank you to ALL the friends and supporters of TC's Forever Home. Everything we do is made possible by you.

The cats we have brought into our home, been able to save and share our lives with, are indebted to you as much as they are us. I can't begin to tell you how awesome you all are.

This book is dedicated to you.

Contents

Introduction

Hi, my name is Kaylen and I am a pragmatic cat man.

Right from the get go, I want to establish how I differentiate between the terms 'Crazy cat man' and the more accurate, for me anyway, 'Pragmatic cat man.' 'Crazy' is a word bandied about quite often when referring to the ownership of multiple cats. This is especially evident when the number of cats with which you cohabit starts to exponentially increase. While I understand that a certain amount of mental instability may be involved in such a venture, the least likely attribute required, would be craziness. The ONLY way to live under the same roof as a bunch of conniving and manipulative felines, is to be stark raving sane. Organisation, structure, and routine are all key in maintaining a functioning household. Clearly all of these are completely at odds with being 'crazy.'

A pragmatic approach is needed, you could say.

They say that women feel and men think. Obviously, there are exceptions to the rule but broadly speaking, I believe this to be true. The truth of this theory becomes very apparent when it comes to the care of animals. For example, a woman may 'feel' that little Tiddles is a bundle of fluffy joy who has walked paw in hand with that woman throughout her life. Tiddles has supported her through trials and tribulations - a confidante and soul-mate. Whereas a man may 'think' that Tiddles is a malevolent, murderous little reprobate who would happily chow down on your still warm flesh should you happen to pass away in your sleep. A man would also 'think' that Tiddles shouldn't be discounted as a suspect if the death in question looked in any way suspicious.

Perhaps though, the truth lies in the muddied waters of both approaches to sharing your life with a cat(s). Seriously though, my first enquiry would be to find out Tiddles' whereabouts at the time of death and whether Tiddles has a rock-solid alibi.

This book has been several years in the writing, ideas happily bubbling away in the slow cooker of my mind with content perpetually being added and other bits dismissed. Even the title has gone under several revisions. Early working titles included 'All cats are bastards,' 'All cats are assholes' or the catchy 'I have now ingested enough cat hair to knit socks for all the feet in a small village.' But none of them quite seemed right. I needed a title that would encapsulate who I am, where I was coming from and my particular approach to 'owning' a cat(s). Yes, yes, I know. We don't own cats, they own us. But for the sake of the narrative, I will use the word 'own' and will happily substitute it for something else when they start paying bed and board.

Dear reader, lest you think I am some kind of cat-hating fiend, I should stress at this early juncture that my love for cats is all encompassing, passionate and genuine. It's just that I am fully aware they are a species predominantly made up of freeloading selfish bastards. They know I know this. I know they know I know this. They know I know they know I know this. It's merely a case of who blinks first. Which of course, will be me. Never have a staring contest with a cat, you will never win.

For your education and entertainment (and as a cathartic exercise for my ongoing and much needed therapy) I aim to document how I went from simply owning 'a' cat to running a fully-fledged cat sanctuary that specialises in giving a forever home to cats that in most cases, the world has simply turned their back on. And indeed, some that just have a bad attitude, causing the world to turn their back. And run.

It's been a journey alright. A piss-drenched, puke-covered, cat hair in my food, poo-fest type of journey. But a journey nonetheless.

Please allow me to share with you - the story of 'The Pragmatic Cat Man.'

Kaylen Fletcher – June 2021

Historical Note

In 1942 on the East bank of the Jordan river, a young Bedouin shepherd who had been out on the lash with his mates, was taking a short cut home when a sand storm arose and he promptly got lost. Blindly flailing about, he tripped over his own inebriated feet and fortuitously stumbled through a bush that had grown over the entrance of a small cave. Unable to see in the dark but grateful to be out of the storm, he curled up and went to sleep. He awoke to the morning light filtering through the now partially exposed cave entrance and took in his surroundings. To his still booze-addled amazement, he discovered that he was surrounded by dozens of niches that had been chiselled out of the living rock and each one contained old and dusty scrolls and parchments. His first thought was that there might be some kind of numerical remuneration for such a find and whether it may help offset the ass whooping he was going to get from his dad for not coming home. He took the scrolls out of their nooks and placed them in the kibr he used as a tote sack. Whistling a cheerful tune, he made his way home.

And so, the young Bedouin passes from the history books without even leaving his name or any news of whether his dad whooped his ass or not. But the story doesn't end there.

Some years later, the scrolls made their way to the leading historical and religious theologians of the day and the great debate began. So, what was in these old, musty scrolls, and what was it that garnered such a kerfuffle? The contents of the scrolls contained an alternative, hitherto unseen, version of the book of Genesis. At this point, you may be asking yourself what any of this has to do with cats? Well, interestingly, at no point are cats mentioned in the bible (that's true). Despite living alongside man for many thousands of years, they don't get a single mention. Nothing. Zip. Nada. These scrolls went some way to addressing this feline-free conundrum.

I should state that, even though the greatest minds the world has to offer have studied these scrolls, as only proper egg heads can, no conclusive agreement has ever been reached as to the authenticity of the content. Therefore, to date, they have not been included in the official bible canon. The debate continues to rage with the 'yay' camp saying the content should be added, and the 'nay' camp saying it should be disregarded as the worst kind of blasphemy. Personally, I think the latter are just dog people, who do get a mention in the bible. (Also true…. Dogs that is, not dog people). I will let you, dear reader, decide for yourself.

The following is the complete and unabridged translation from the original manuscripts; we join it at Genesis chapter 1, verse 24….

24 And God said, let the earth bring forth the living creature after his kind, cattle, and creeping thing, and beast of the earth after his kind: and it was so.

25 And God made the beast of the earth after his kind, and cattle after their kind, and everything that creepeth upon the earth after his kind: and God saw that it was good.

26 And God said, let us make man in our image, after our likeness: and let them have dominion over the fish of the sea, and over the fowl of the air, and over the cattle, and over all the earth, and over every creeping thing that creepeth upon the earth.

27 And Satan said, (remember at this time Satan was still a high-ranking angel) 'Ere boss, can I 'ave a go?

God: What do you mean my son, 'ave a go'?

Satan: Ya know, creatin' an' stuff.

God: Well, I'm not sure....

Jesus: Father...can I have a word?

God: Certainly, my son.

Jesus: *whispers* Father some of the angels have been talking....and um....

God: Go ahead, my son.

Jesus: Well, it's just at breaktime down in the canteen, some of Satan's ideas and views are a bit....

God: Holy? Too pious? Too selfless?

Jesus: No, not exactly... more subversive, treacherous, and evil.

God: Come now my son, I'm sure he is just high spirited and forward thinking.

Jesus: He tries to put his hand up the vending machine flap and grab chocolate without paying.

God: No more of this Jesus. Perhaps a little creation work will do young Satan the world of good.

God: Satan my son, come hence.

Satan: Yes boss?

God: I am entrusting in you great responsibility.

Satan: I'm on it, boss.

God: This is not a task to be embarked on lightly.

Satan: I got this boss.

God: It will need to reflect kindness and beauty.

Satan: Yeah, no worries, easy-peasy.

And so, it was that the angel Satan went out unto the earth and did create stuff. On the seventh day, he did return unto the presence of his Lord and laid down his creation as an offering at his master's feet.

Satan: Well then boss, whattaya reckon?

God: It's.... umm.... very nice, Satan. What is it?

Satan: It's a cat, innit?

God: Okay. What exactly does it do?

Satan: Well...it sleeps and stuff.'

God: And stuff?

Satan: *mumbles incoherently*

God: Sorry I didn't catch that?

Satan: Umm, well, it kills things.

God: Kills?

Satan: Yeah. Nuffin you'd miss, like. Mice, spider. Ya slippers....

God: I WILL NOT HAVE ANYTHING THAT KIL....

Satan: Stroke it.

God: Sorry, what?

Satan: Pick it up and stroke it.

God: Well, I'm not sure but I suppose.... It just bit me!

Satan: That means it likes you. Stroke it.

God: I fail to see.... Oh, this is soft.

Satan: It's good for what ails you master.

God: What is that delightful noise it's making?

Satan: That's a purr, yer honour.

God: Oh. What purpose does that serve?

Satan: Nuffin really.

God: Well, my son, I see you have put a lot of thought into this but.... oh, it's jumped down.

Satan: Cat stuff to do, milord. Highly intelligent creatures are cats.

God: It's just been sick on the carpet!

Satan: Sorry about that guvnor.... Still a bit of fine tuning to do. Gremlins to iron out so to speak....

God: No, my son. Whilst I appreciate the time and effort you have put into this 'cat,' it will not do at all. It does not fit with the peace and harmony of this beautiful paradise I have creat…. where did it go?

Satan: 'Boss?'

God: It was here one second and now it's gone!

Satan: Sneaky bastards, cats. Got to watch them.

God: Satan, please tell me you didn't leave the door open?

Satan: Ummm….

God: Ah bugger….

Chapter 1 - We Weren't Allowed A Dog

Meet Mattie...this gorgeous wee girl turned up in the fields around our house having possibly been dumped. After a frustrating couple of hours, we managed to trap her and then whisk her off to the vets for a health check. Fortunately, she passed with flying colours. Being semi-feral, the chances are she will never be a lap cat but loves love on her own terms and has set up camp on the window sill in our hallway.

Well, we weren't. Despite vigorously working on the weak link in my parents' marriage (mum), dad was adamant that we would not be having a dog. Whether or not this is a type of parental abuse, I will leave for the reader to decide. But as a young child, this type of tyrannical ruling seemed immensely unfair. At the time, I seem to recall he used puerile objections such as, "You'll forget to feed it, let alone take it for walks."

Whether such nonsense protestations would have proven to be true or not is a moot point, as the 'getting of a dog' never came to pass. He did, however, compromise and we were allowed a rabbit. This was mostly rubbish. Snowball did literally nothing all day long, apart from nibble stuff and occasionally bite me. Some of my earliest memories are of cleaning her hutch out on a Saturday mor⬛⬛⬛⬛⬛⬛⬛⬛⬛⬛⬛tch HAD TO BE DONE. The smel⬛⬛⬛⬛⬛⬛⬛⬛⬛⬛⬛⬛d straw haunts me still. But this⬛⬛⬛⬛⬛⬛⬛⬛⬛⬛⬛ut cats.

At some p⬛⬛⬛⬛⬛⬛⬛⬛⬛⬛⬛as agreed a cat would join the fa⬛⬛⬛⬛⬛⬛⬛⬛⬛⬛stly better than a rubbish rabbit.⬛⬛⬛⬛⬛⬛⬛⬛⬛

We got Sa⬛⬛⬛⬛⬛⬛⬛⬛⬛ssibly a witch) who had the mos⬛⬛⬛⬛⬛⬛⬛⬛⬛d whose house smelt very stron⬛⬛⬛⬛⬛⬛⬛⬛een quite young as I don't remem⬛⬛⬛⬛⬛⬛⬛⬛om him being a big ginger Tom ⬛⬛⬛⬛⬛⬛⬛⬛at the house he came from that smelt of wee. Sorry for the pathetic recollections Sargent but it is what it is.

Next came a dark tortoiseshell called Smokie who had lost half her tail in a gin trap. I seem to recollect that she just turned up one day and we started feeding her. She was an affectionate creature and decided to live with us. Smokie had a litter of kittens and we kept one that we named Tiptoes. For the life of me, I have no idea who came up with that name. He certainly didn't walk on tiptoes. It was probably my little sister and we were just lucky he wasn't called princess. She was obsessed with princesses. Tiptoes was a male calico, which is highly unusual, and he was present for the majority of my formative and teenage years. Tiptoes holds the honour of being the first cat I can say that I properly remember.

Both sets of grandparents also had cats. Not a single dog in sight for a cherubic sweet grandchild like myself to love and pet. Even if this whole lack of 'doggieness' in my extended family can't exactly be classed as abuse, at the very least, it was cruel and mean. Let's not quibble over semantics, dear reader, it was definitely abuse. I digress. From a very early age, we differentiated between the sets of grandparents by their cats' names. Dad's parents had a cat called Fifi whilst mum's parents had a cat called Cocoa.

And so, visits were announced as "Kids we are going to see Fifi's nana and grandad." This was always a time of great rejoicing as dad's parents were richer and the standard of gift received was much better. Granny would always palm us money and without fail we would return home with a tube of Smarties.

OR

"Kids we are going to see Cocoa's Nana and Grandad." Collective groans usually accompanied this announcement, as this nan was always moaning. The only 'gift' we would bring home, was maybe a clipped ear from my grumpy grandad. It was the seventies after all, and men being complete bastards was an issue that was still barely frowned upon.

The point I guess I'm trying to make is that, as a family, we always had cats around. They were part of the fixtures and fittings in our home, literally like a piece of furniture. Albeit a piece of furniture that on occasion would leave a smelly deposit on a carelessly discarded piece of school uniform.

***

Wackadoodle was the first cat that was just mine. For a while in my life, it was just him and me and me and him. He was/is just the most awesome, handsome boy. He's the cover boy by the way. That look on his face is, I like to think, his way of saying "This is my human". And in many ways, that's exactly what I am.

Our bond started very early in his life. That is to say, right at the beginning. I was visiting a friend and, during the time I was visiting, their existing cat went into labour in the bottom of her wardrobe. I realised that she was struggling to bite through the umbilical cord (the mama cat not my friend) of one of her kittens. The cord had wrapped itself tightly around the kitten's neck. After some frantic googling, I manfully stepped up and cut it for her. Some people may wish to call me a hero. I appreciate that is a robust term to use about me but feel free to use it nonetheless. Anyone?

There were three kittens in the litter, Wackadoodle, as he was soon named, and his two pretty little sisters. The two girls were postcard perfect with symmetrical markings so they were destined to sail through life based solely on their looks. And possibly repeat fees from Felix adverts.

Doodle was what I would have termed 'fugly'. In hindsight perhaps it was a little cruel to call him that but he was a thorn betwixt two roses. A Munch 'tween a couple of Monet's. A stale digestive on a plate next to a couple of chocolate Hobnobs. Since I could identify with the feeling of being a stale old biscuit myself at times, when it came to rehoming the kittens, I knew I just couldn't be parted from the 'Doodle'.

Right from the start Wacka, the name which he goes by on a daily basis, was what you can only term a 'yappy' cat. He was always very popular with visitors to my house because of the way he would circulate, individually chatting, seemingly conducting full-on conversations. In reality, he is no different than any other cat. He is simply demanding something and merely repeating himself to his audience, incessantly, until they get off their ass and get or do whatever it is the cat requires/demands. To the uninitiated though, it does sound cute and make them feel wanted.

When Wacka was a couple of months old, I started a job that involved 12-hour shifts, night and day, and I realised that my boy was used to seeing a lot of me. So, I decided that a companion might be in order. As it happened, a friend of mine had a semi-feral cat that had recently had a litter of kittens.... And so, shortly afterwards, a little black terror we subsequently called Hodor, joined the family. Right from the start they were the best of friends. They would madly play 'chase' around the house, doing their best to wreck the joint in a way that only people who have had two kittens at the same can really relate to. Despite being the younger of the two, Hodor soon emerged as the boss, with Wacka as the more than willing side-kick. They were completely inseparable and often of a night, I would pull slowly in to my driveway after a long shift at work, to see Hodor scoot by in the glare of my headlights, invariably with Wacka hard at his heels. It was a great friendship to witness and more than assuaged my guilt at working such long hours. Sadly, one night only Wacka appeared in the beam of my car lights and I instantly knew something was amiss. I searched all the local roads and questioned my neighbours but Hodor had simply disappeared and I never saw him again. I take some small consolation that because a body never turned up, maybe somebody picked him up, perhaps thinking him a stray (I don't hold with collars) and even as I type this, he is now a big black tom, stretched out somewhere in front of a roaring fire, with a stomach full of cooked chicken. Who's to say he isn't?

I know Wacka missed his friend at first but life goes on. With typical cat resilience, Wacka was fine. If anything, he was forced to became more of his own man. He would spend more and more time outside, wandering far and wide, often for days at a time. You have to understand that this was a manly house and whilst I knew the responsible thing would be to get Wacka neutered, I stayed my hand because he was obviously having a time of it. He was out sowing his oats and adventuring his little heart out. He was happy and therefore so was I.

Following what can only be termed a 'traumatic' break-up (aren't they all), I felt that I desperately needed a change of scenery and was offered a place to live with a very good friend back across the water in England. This left me with rather a sticky dilemma. The opportunity was almost too good to pass up but the move wouldn't be suitable for my boy, who was now a country cat through and through. I just couldn't take him to an urban environment. Emotionally and mentally, I had been through the wringer. So, after much soul-searching, I came to the conclusion that, on the proviso I could find Wacka a decent and loving home, we would part ways. He could get on with his life and I could get on with reshaping mine.

My efforts to find that 'decent and loving home' led me down an unexpected route and doors I had never anticipated, suddenly swung open before me.

Chapter 2 – It's All In The Name

Meet Artemis.... Artemis lost his human mummy when she was very young and so he came to live with us. Despite having a few behavioural issues (spraying) that we are constantly trying to address, he is one of the friendliest boys you could ever hope to meet. There are lap cats and then there is Artemis, he completely fails to understand or care that you may have stuff to do and would happily stay cuddled up with you all day.

I will pause my tale at this point to address the rather serious issue of naming your new feline companion. I think the best advice I can give you, at the very outset, is to wait a couple of a weeks before naming your new cat or kitten.

On the day you get your cat, you may look down at that little adoring face, those big, innocent, round eyes looking up at you and your brain may scream "My god I have never seen anything so exquisitely perfect. I must call him Mr Fluffy of number 7 Awesome Street, Upper Gorgeousville."

Whereas, a   behaviour for a week or two, you   ight be 'Ivan the Terrible'. Or possi

You have u   nto your house. Yes, it may purr a   utter every time you look at it, bu   the bone. It has claws that may se   s the capacity to completely destr   gurine that has been in your fami

At this poi   om the late Sir Terry Pratchett v   ogs we'd realize what nasty, crue   le. That's what people remember

There is n   although some people still get lucky. I.E. "We shall call him Tiddles!" In all fairness though, that is quite a common prophetic name.

A case which totally proves my point is a little CH cat we got (that stands for cerebellar hypoplasia.... more about that later) that my wife was set on calling Willow. Willow, of course, is a goddamned hippydippy name. During those first couple of weeks, we noticed she had somewhat of an angry face. Somehow the word angry morphed in to 'Angee' and her name has now changed permanently. She is never referred to as Willow. I consider that a lucky escape for her.

You will often find that the given name naturally evolves, often ending up with only a passing acquaintance to the original designation. A particular example that comes to mind is our lovely big boy Benson.

Who wasn't addressed as such for at least 8 years.

Most commonly he was called Benny. Often, 'Ma big son'. Sometimes, 'Benamin'. On occasion, 'Benjamin Netanyahu'. Every now and then, he would even be addressed as, "I was gonna have that pork chop for my dinner ya bastard. Go and eat from your own plate!"

In a nut shell, I'm saying be 'fluid' about your cat's name.

Another consideration you may wish to take into account is how your cat's name will fit in to a song. Stop laughing and let me explain.

Invariably, at some point, you will compose a song about your cat. The tune in question will almost certainly mention their names and quite possibly some of their finer attributes. The lyrics may end up being a touch banal and you may find it necessary to crowbar words in to make it rhyme, but YOU WILL make up a song at some stage.

Whilst the finished melody may not have garnered you a favourable comment from Simon Cowell on the X-Factor, it will delight your cat. As you know, all cats are narcissists and after all, the song is all about them.

Here is one I composed for our beautiful little Beans.

'Beans Beans Beans ba dooby dooby'

'Beans Beans Beans ba dooby dooby'

'Beans Beans Beans ba dooby dooby'

'Beans Beans Beans ba dooby dooby'

'Beans Beans Beans ba dooby dooby'

'Beans Beans Beans ba dooby dooby'

Yes, yes, yes, it's a little repetitive but it works perfectly with a 12-bar blues. And Beans loves it.

Whilst sharing a refrain with your little furry buddy is both a personal and bonding experience, I found it to be somewhat of a mood dependant thing. Sometimes the last thing you want to do is express your feelings through the medium of song if the little bastard has just shat on the carpet.

Something else you may wish to consider, if you are particularly blessed, is that your furry may be with you for a very long time. 20 years isn't beyond the realms of possibility these days. So, you may need to consider that your chosen name ought to be something that stands the test of time.

Picture the scene, dear reader. The year is 2040 and the world's natural resources are nearly depleted. People will literally kill for a corned-beef sandwich. Flying cars fill the skies. And you're on your doorstep calling for Cardi B. I have nothing against Cardi B, but you get my point.

The names of our crew have, so far, either been of my choice (the cool ones), my wife's choosing (meh) or ones that we have come to some semblance of agreement on (i.e., my wife had the final say).

Personally, I like funny and unusual names. I mean come on.... Wackadoodle? Among the names I have been 'allowed' so far have been Bandit, Peanut, Bongo, Toots, Scrummy, Donut, Beans, Pootle, and Pom-Pom. I have, however, been denied Bagel. My wife, for some reason, will not countenance the name Bagel regardless of how much I cajole and wheedle. A cat, somewhere out there, needs to be called Bagel. Please take this name with my blessing, as my gift to you.

Another thing you may wish to consider, are those inevitable vet visits. Vets have developed the practice of announcing your pet's name out loud when it comes to your turn to be seen. If you are sat there with a massive Rottweiler and they holler "Tyson please", nobody blinks an eye and you can happily and proudly strut across the waiting area with your magnificent specimen of an animal. They may or may not applaud in appreciation.

If, however, you have an overweight, cantankerous tabby called Princess Lovelybottom, this type of announcement from the vet may be a cause for embarrassment. Personally, I don't have a problem with this, as the vet is the one who has to make the proclamatic   s reactions when it's a particularly silly nam   pretended not to hear so they have to call   this advice is coming from someone who h   ot covered in cat hair for the last seven ye   scious is something way back in the rear-   UT, don't say I didn't warn you.

I hope this cha   little when it comes to naming your pros   reflection, the whole chapter is probably m   of the time, your cat will ignore you when you call it by its name anyway.

Chapter 3 - How I Bagged A Crazy Cat Lady

Meet Xander.... full name Xander Handsome-pants. This beautiful boy had an horrific start to life, coming from a litter of kittens that had suffered some of the worst abuse I have ever heard of. Understandably, he is incredibly wary of humans and only bonded with Ali in the early stages of his life. It took me a full 5 years to win his trust and get to the point where he was confident that daddy wouldn't hurt him and, in fact, gives great snuggles. He is still incredibly shy around visitors to the house. Xander spends his day exploring the fields around our house or can be found fast asleep on his mum's pillow.

With still a certain amount of time to play out before my big move, I decided to put myself 'out there' a little. My reasoning behind this was that one could never have too many friends. I was also hoping for a little boost to my flagging self-confidence. With this as my objective, I joined a popular networking site. As well as offering romantic entanglements, this site had a feature for making relationships of a more 'platonic' nature. It was perhaps a little naïve on my behalf not to realise that this 'feature' was quite common with homosexuals who weren't looking for 'anything serious'. I'm flattered to say that I received a little attention from some rather amiable gay chaps and indeed some who thought they could 'change my mind'. But no, this man was not for turning. In fact, I literally ended up apologising to one chap responding that "Sorry buddy, I just like boobs too much and men are way too hairy."

As my profile picture for this site, I had used the beautiful photo that adorns the front cover of this book and, while I dodged the odd advances of random gay fellas, I managed to catch the attention of a certain Alicat666. It was something like that anyway. I say 'I' caught her attention. But, in truth, it was the handsome boy sat on my lap that had intrigued her. Her very first message was actually to ask me what he was called. Quickly checking her profile, I saw that she too had pictures of her cats. And so it was I started to devise a cunning plan.

Her name was Ali. Over the course of the week immediately following that first message, we spoke on the phone a fair bit. We built up somewhat of a rapport and, consequently, decided to meet in person at a popular coffee house. In our telephone conversations, I had tentatively bought up the subject of my imminent move and the dire need of a good home for Wacka. Even though she had politely, but firmly, refused, stating that her "7 cats were more than a responsibility enough", I secretly hoped that if we met in person, I could 'grease the wheels' as it were. I could present my case and throw in a little charm to boot. With hindsight, knowing this woman the way I do now, there is no way I would have considered such a stupidly manipulative and indeed 'male' approach. But that was then and I was an idiot.

It's always slightly nerve-wracking when you meet someone for the first time, especially so when you are in need of a big favour and the recipient of said favour is a tattoo covered vision of beauty. I actually love to recount to close friends and family my first impression of seeing Ali. She had arrived before me and was happily ordering herself a coffee and sandwich. She was standing side on to me as I walked through the door and she didn't initially notice me. I can still vividly remember feeling like my legs were going to buckle and I was torn between nonchalantly, in a fake nonchalant type way, either just walking in or turning tail and legging it. But she was just so damned pretty. I figured that I could run, throw my phone out of the car window, destroy my computer and, as I hadn't told her my address, it would be the perfect getaway. However, I pulled myself together and reminded myself I was there for Wackadoodle, pretty face or not.

My nerves were somewhat misplaced because, as soon as I got Ali's attention and introductions were made, normality kicked in and we chatted away like the friends we had become over the previous week's correspondence. In all honesty, I forget much of what we talked about that afternoon. I do, however, remember that she had to repeatedly open the number-coded toilet door for me, as I have massive sausage fingers and I kept forgetting the code. I remember she showed me many of her cat inspired tattoos. I remember we talked a lot about cats. I remember the conversation ebbed and flowed in just the most natural way. Most of all, I remember it was over all too soon.

I'm pretty sure we talked about her rehoming Wacka, in a half-hearted, vague sort of way. I'm also pretty sure she still refused. But all of a sudden, that wasn't the most important issue of the day. Despite my better judgement, my thorough conviction of the path my life was due to take, I had messed everything up and fallen in love with her. Such a bloke thing to do I hear you say. Well, you weren't there, I couldn't help it. It's entirely her fault. She cast a spell with that witchy witchiness every woman possesses to varying degrees. I was merely a fly caught in her web of womanly wiles. I never stood a chance.

The drive home was a happy, dream-like affair. For the whole trip, I wondered what was going to happen next?

***

Over the days that followed, we texted and chatted on the phone and we made arrangements for me to go and see her at her house in Belfast. I didn't quite have the heightened nerves this time around but I was still a little apprehensive and a little worried that a woman who shared her home with 7 cats might not quite be the goddess my overactive imagination had made her out to be. Frankly, I was worried her house might smell of piss.

My preconceptions of how crazy cat ladies actually managed to survive in a house infested with felines, were blown away when Ali opened her front door. I was greeted by the scent of sweet-smelling candles, not piss. She invited me into her clean, neat, and tidy two up two down and I couldn't help but think I was going to have a major clean-up of MY house before I ever let her set foot over the doorstep. And I only had one cat. Well one cat and me. It's fair to say our mess was 50/ 50.

Almost immediately, I was introduced to her furry family and Ali fired all their names at me as she picked each one up, kissing them and extolling their many quirks and virtues. In that moment, it dawned on me that it was of the utmost importance for me to learn their names, and quickly. To be humming and hawing over who was who in six months' time would not do at all. The importance of this felt like it would be a deal breaker. Seven names you say? Easy! Not so. The bloody things kept moving about and to confuse matters, several of them had similar markings and colours. I resolved that on my next visit, I would bring a notepad and discreetly jot down pertinent and discernible differences between them all.

The rest of the evening was simply lovely. We had both deep and light-hearted conversations, worked out what we had in common and what made us different. The whole time I was while being alternately walked or sat on by the more inquisitive and bolder cats. Don't get me wrong, the schemas in my head as to what a crazy cat lady would be like, were not all inaccurate. There was definitely a 'cat theme' going on in the house in terms of the art, ornaments etc. But none of the negative connotations I had anticipated were true. Even the litter trays were discreetly placed.

As the evening wore on, I think we both knew there was a certain 'something' between us and that there were possibilities in the air. It was late, and after agreeing that we would take things slow, she agreed to let me stay over. Of course, this was on the proviso that it would be 'chaste'. And it was. And I cared not a bit. It was big picture time for me.

Someone else's bed is never the same as your own, and you never quite get that great night's sleep that you would enjoy at home. Consequently, I was awake very early. Barely conscious, and only half remembering where I was, I was torn between getting up for a wee and trying my best not to disturb Ali. I lay there for a while trying to gather my befuddled wits and I couldn't help but notice there was a distinct lack of another human breathing beside me, but there was noise coming from downstairs. It was the type of noise someone makes when they're trying really hard not to make a noise. I tentatively groped around the bed to make sure I was indeed alone. I was, so I made the executive decision to bite the bullet and get up. Feeling ever so much the stranger in a strange house, I made my way down the stairs, where I could hear Ali whispering away to the cats. I sheepishly stuck my head around the doorframe, cleared my throat, and said good morning. Ali, in the middle of the morning feed, saw that as her cue to end social convention and boomed "Good morning". She then proceeded to outline her daily morning routine. My very worst fear had come true. She was a morning person. The whole thing is a horrible blur but I remember the above scenario took place at some ungodly hour. It was at least 5 am. Well, it may not have been 5 but it was certainly before 8.

I realised that if there was to be any chance of a future relationship between us, certain ground rules had to be established. Firstly, I was incapable of coherent thought or speech before a cup of coffee and a minimum of two cigarettes. Secondly, if I was to put my hands round her throat and tightly squeeze, it was because she was being too 'chirpy' and therefore would have nobody to blame but herself. Funny thing is, it transpired she's not a morning person either; it's just that she keeps milkman hours and her morning is about 5 hours before mine.

After my caffeine and nicotine hits, I was starting to feel a little more human but still secretly feared there might be a sudden pop quiz on the cats' names. Throwing out 'Tiddles' or 'Mr Fluffy' may have appeased a lay cat person but, to the true cat lover, this would have been an affront to the dignity of her 'children' and surely have seen me out on my ear. Thankfully, Ali just chatted away about how she got up early every morning between 3.30 and 5.... Pretty twisted huh? She had done this for as long as she could remember. The time was utilised to feed the cats, clean and bleach the litter trays, clean the house from top to bottom, and then groom and play with the cats. If that wasn't enough, in her spare time, she volunteered at the local Cats Protection branch and did it all again for cats that weren't even hers!

I guess it was on that first morning when my proper 'cat education' truly began. I think many people (I say this with increased insight, include myself, and am ashamed to admit it) that we do see animals as lesser species and view them in terms of what they can do for us, as opposed to what we can do for them. Strangely, I was completely fascinated by what Ali was telling me.

Living in a small(ish) house, with so many little bodies running around, it was imperative that there was a semblance of order and that peace among them should be a priority. Ali would give each equal attention, no one was ever neglected and behavioural issues were dealt with firmly and quickly. For instance, did you know the importance of such things as the order they are fed in? That you should always have more beds than cats, so that they always have a choice? That you should promptly clean the litter trays? That you should make sure the cats have enough space, make sure they have enough privacy etc.?

I swear, it's a science all by itself.

Having lived this life for so long, Ali almost has superhuman powers. I swear she can hear a cat take a dump in a litter tray from half a mile away. She knows who's doing it and what its consistency will be.

I digress.

I remember driving home that day, mulling over in my mind what a completely unique individual I had gotten involved with. Her passion was infectious and I felt a door had opened before me to a world I knew very little of but wanted to know lots more about. It was clear that Ali was a package deal and that any romantic overtures of a serious nature would be reciprocated only if the cats were part and parcel of it. It really didn't take that much thinking about.

Over the following months, we got to know each other much better and, equally importantly, I got to know her kids (get used to that expression, we seldom refer to them as cats and NEVER as pets) names and their personalities. Not only that but

I learned their likes and dislikes and who I could safely pick up without fear of my face being clawed off.

Shortly afterwards, we made a joint decision that travelling between our respective homes was a complete pain in the ass, costly, and ⬛ r mine and so, we decided to combine ⬛ in a house in the country, surrounde ⬛ the best interests of everyone if they ⬛ at's exactly what happened.

Chapter 4 – The Three 'P's

Meet Banoo…full name Anna Banana Banoo. She is stone deaf and a complete destructive loon. Single-handedly, she has wrecked more stuff in the house than all the other cats put together. She will happily climb on your shoulder for some upfront and personal love and if you're really lucky sink her teeth in to the end of your nose. Banoo is batshit crazy and we love her all the more for it.

Now, before any of you get carried away with romantic notions of running a cat sanctuary all of your own; of lazy afternoons with your feet up watching Netflix whilst surrounded by adoring pussies, I feel I need to give you a sharp, hard, metaphorical slap around the face. Literal slaps available on request. This is probably the most IMPORTANT chapter of the whole book, so fail to take heed at your own peril.

The three 'P's.' More commonly known as Poo, Piss and Puke.

For the sake of the narrative, we will lump hairballs with puke as they are just a type of barf anyway. I CANNOT stress enough how all three will become an integral part of your life, your being, and your nightmares. Ask anyone who shares their home with even one cat and how they cope with the deposits it emits from its various orifices. Then, times that by 20 and you are now venturing in to one of Dante's circles of hell. A hell, that is, in which you must not walk barefoot....

***

Poo

Cats poo a lot and not always handily in your neighbour's vegetable patch as you would wish them to. For the sake of fairness SOME cats will ALWAYS poo outside, bury it neatly and you are none the wiser to your beloved companion's bowel movements. Whereas others are holy terrors and like nothing better than taking a nice squirty motion in your favourite slippers.

That's right I said squirty. Only in your wildest dreams does a cat consistently and regularly produce an offering that resembles something like a dried fig. In fact, I pray for dry figs. Alongside the heady heights of dry 'figgishness,' you may experience smelly water, smelly gloopy water, slightly more solid gloop, glistening fig then dry fig.

The 'dry fig' is what we all desire, dear reader.

Of course, if you are faced with a puddle of anything from smelly water to slightly solid gloop, you can't just ignore it. You will, or ought to, ask yourself why? In the same way as it would in a human, a stool sample is a picture that paints a thousand words. It's a picture that you probably wouldn't want to hang up in your house but colour and consistency can tell you a lot about your cat's health. Often, it may be something as simple as your cat needing to be wormed or it has eaten something that doesn't agree with it. A lot of cats will happily munch down on road kill just as eagerly as they will enjoy that £2 a tin, super-duper stuff you treat them to. A cat with constant loose bowels is not a good thing and he needs looking at so get your ass (and its) to the vets.

Piss

Beyond a shadow of a doubt by FAR the worst of the three P's.

It's smelly, it can run under things and the smell can't half linger.

'Spraying' in particular can be very problematic. If I could give one tip, from our experience, it's that a male kitten should be neutered BEFORE it reaches sexual maturity - around 4 months is good. That is the stage where spraying can become a habit. Many people think that the simple act of neutering a tom will stop it from spraying but, alas, that isn't always the case. If a cat starts spraying, there's every chance it will continue to spray even after being neutered, because it has developed a behaviour. Undoing that behaviour is extremely difficult. In fact, when it comes to behavioural problems 'spraying' is up there as one of the worst. Owners literally try everything and tear their hair out, not only to stop the problem but to get rid of the resulting smell.

Piddle can, like poo, be potentially indicative of underlying problems, both health and behavioural. If a normally continent cat starts weeing around the house in particular places or at random, you can be looking at a puss that is maybe stressed or has kidney problems. Again, if in any doubt get yourselves to the vet.

Perhaps the biggest revelation to me concerning widdle, has been the sheer corrosive aspect of it. We are talking industrial paint-stripper here. In my house alone, I have had to replace skirting and floorboards that have been eaten way by that evil yellow brew. Again, a handy tip on eliminating that errant urine is to mop up the worst of it and clean the area with a diluted biological washing powder solution. That will hopefully break down the ammonia – the component that creates the stubborn whiff and encourages repeat offences.

Like it or not, if you are aiming to have a multi-cat household, then pee is something you are going to have to deal and live with. Many an evening in our home the dreaded "Can you smell piss?" question can be heard, followed by two grown adults on their hands and knees, bums in the air, sniffing the perimeter of the room for that elusive discharge.

Puke (and fur-balls).

You have had a wonderful evening, enjoyed a fine meal, and maybe enjoyed an excellent film and you have just got in to a lovely freshly made, warm bed. Who knows, the stars may have aligned and to put a cherry on the top of a perfect night your partner is feeling amorous and the chances of jiggy are looking to be guaranteed. Then 'that' noise begins.

'That' noise that only a person who has lived with a cat knows. Knows and dreads.

'That' noise, and excuse my onomatopoeic skills here, sounding something like....

"Woer...woer...woer...woer...woer...ack!"

Any thought, hopes or dreams of lustful shenanigans are quickly dismissed as covers are thrown back. And, with speed that would put Usain Bolt to shame, you rush to find the gagging culprit. The aim of the exercise is obviously to get to the cat before it reaches the 'ack' part of this ghastly drama. Even if you do, you are then presented with the problem of what to do next. Whereas, my wife will lovingly stroke its back whilst making soothing noises, my reaction is somewhat more practical. Depending on location I will either put the cat in the sink or take it none too languidly to the front door, where it can desecrate the garden all it likes. Meanwhile, I blearily question my life choices and once again consider becoming a Sherpa in Peru. Ninety-nine times out of a hundred though, you will not reach the cat pre 'ack.' Another interesting fact is that approximately ninety-five times out of a hundred, your beloved companion will have been sick in your slippers.

ONCE AGAIN, a puking puss may be indicating an underlying health problem. If it becomes a regular thing, then get him/her checked out. Most often, this is not the case. Your boking buddy may simply have eaten something that did not agree with him/her or was simply curious as to how quick you would be to respond from being stone-cold asleep to feverishly wide awake.

Oh, I could wax lyrical for hours about the three 'P's, the colours, the smells, the nightmares and so on. But, if I still have your attention dear reader, then you are probably already accustomed to them, a delusional idealist or maybe possess just a little masochistic quirk in your nature. As for me I have rescinded my responsibility on the matter and once again you have been warned!

Chapter 5 – The New Regime

Meet Maisie.... Little Miss Maisie-Moo Bobble-Head. This wee dote is simply an angel fallen from above. Maisie has CH, explained later in the book, but has an indomitable lust for life and adventure. She has a very deep bond with her mummy and, although now 2 years old, is still not much bigger than a kitten. Every guest who visits instantly falls in love with her.

I live in a 200-year-old farm house. It's slightly damp and the money required to heat it would bankroll a small country. Having sold my spleen (not really, because that's illegal) to achieve even a modicum of warmth in the house, it would only ever really reach the ambient temperature of your standard fridge but I'm happy enough to put on another jumper. The property itself is ideal for the discerning feline, because it includes numerous old barns and out-buildings that are full of dark hidey holes. These buildings house a plethora of small rodents, spiders, and birds. In addition, the house is surrounded by rolling fields which, for much of the year, are covered in long grass. This grass makes the fields into a hunter's paradise for four-legged furries who are that way inclined. My home is secluded and private, oozes charm and character. It's my castle and my sanctum, and I love it.

Sadly though, Ali was not equally enthralled.

Some of the more hurtful remarks etched into my mind are related to the orange kitchen I had at the time. Come on, it was retro. The dirt on my light-switches was deep enough to grow spuds (they may have been a tad grubby). My music room "had to go!"

*Side note - Had I been able to sing and possessed more than a passing competence at playing the guitar, I could have been the next Leo Sayer.

Despite ALL of this, Ali being who she is, chose to put the cats first. She saw the potential of what this unique environment could mean for them. So, she declared herself happy to make the transition and move in with Wacka and me.

It was late January when Ali and the gang came to live with us and I recall the previous weeks being a mad flurry of cleaning and decorating. Keen and eager to impress, I even spruced up areas that had hitherto seldom witnessed the sight of mop or cloth. Like underneath the toilet seat. I remember feeling more than just a bit little hard done by when Ali made a military type inspection of my sanitation efforts and found them wanting. It was a happy outcome all round though as she went round the house and did it all again 'properly.'

With many of these little teething problems being addressed, as happens when any two families come together, we then confronted my approach to cat care. Which was, of course, all wrong.

The first issue that commanded her attention was that of Wackadoodle's testicles.

Those, I was informed, needed removing at the first available opportunity. My poor boy had not only opened his furry arms wide in welcome to these interlopers but now had to sacrifice his wrinklepurse. A little unfair I suppose, but then again, I had been forced to repaint my kitchen. As a now seasoned cat carer, I see the absolute importance of neutering/spaying your cat but at the time I felt a little hard done by for my boy. Still, life is about sacrifice, something I now knew from first-hand experience because my orange curtains had to go too.

And then it came to feeding time.

Once again, I felt a little aggrieved that the 'system' I had in operation came under such a blistering attack. It went like this. I would buy a cheap and cheerful dry cat food, fill up a tin bowl and leave it on my front doorstep. When it was empty, I would refill it. Rinse and repeat ad infinitum. Personally, I thought this was an excellent way of doing things and I was also doing my bit for the local wildlife, since the local crows would help themselves. So would an old dog fox who wandered through the yard once a day. I was the Greta Thunberg of my road, you could say.

But Ali absolutely would not have said that.

The first thing she wanted to know was when did I last clean the bowl? Perhaps answering "I can't remember" (I couldn't), wasn't the best thing to say. After recovering from a mini-stroke she hoyed the bowl in to the wheelie bin. This too, upset me a little, as I had formed a sentimental attachment to that little bowl. It was one of those old white and blue enamelled tin ones that had developed a lovely patina of chips and rust over the years. It may even have had some monetary value, as I'm fairly sure it dated back to the Second World War. With hindsight, that may have been the last time it was washed too....

Next to be addressed was 'choice' of food. Eh?

She asked me how I would feel if I had to eat the same thing over and over, day after day? I pointed out that if we were talking about lasagne and chips followed by treacle pudding and custard, then it would be an accommodation I could quite happily live with. She thought I was being facetious (I wasn't) and went on to explain that a wet food diet is better for cats and that a long-term dry food diet isn't great for their kidneys. Offering a choice of food with different flavours etc., was part of having a loving relationship with your cat.

"He can catch a rabbit whenever he wants to", garnered me nothing more than a withering look.

Next...(her) "Where does he sleep?" Eh? Where does he sleep?

I wondered if this was a trick question and could only respond with "Wherever he likes, he's a cat." She was making the point that I didn't have any cat-specific beds, which I found a little strange as I thought a cat could consider anything to be a bed. After all, I have literally seen Wackadoodle fast asleep in a shoe. Retrieving my now decidedly overworked credit card from my wallet (let's not forget I had already had to repaint my lovely orange kitchen), we fitted out all the windowsills with nice new comfy beds with a few others thrown in besides. This was in case the cats 'fancied a change.' Once again, I pointed out that I had just the one chair (my dad's old electric recliner) and I was more than happy with it. I neither required nor wanted a 'choice'. With hindsight, I shouldn't have drawn her attention to my chair as a point to further my argument, as that 'had to go' as well.

Next, she wanted to know where we should place all the litter trays? Eh?

"Obviously, we will have some in the bathroom", she blithely continued, "but I think we should have some others 'scattered around' seeing as the bathroom is at the end of the house and that's quite a long way to go for the older ones."

Now you must understand, dear reader, that this suggestion in particular left me completely nonplussed, as we live in the middle of the countryside. As far as I was aware, cats considered the entire world their toilet. "What need do they have for litter trays at all?" I reasoned'.

Here's the thing about Ali, and she is a complete bastard for this, she loves comparing cats to humans. If we are ever having a discussion/argument about the cats and in particular if she is losing the discussion/argument about the cats, she will pull this tactic out of her ass. For example, the then litter tray 'discussion' where I had brilliantly offered my 'the world is a toilet' rebuttal, was settled with the rhetorical (she loves a good rhetorical does Ali) question.

"And would you like to go to toilet outside all year round?"

If someone uses this type of logic as a baseline for their arguments, a mere mortal like my humble self stands no chance. Even as I ventured "I often have a widdle outside when I'm gardening", I knew the discussion was over. One withering look and one unwanted rhetorical question answered later, we moved on to the subject of sleeping arrangements.

"What sleeping arrangements? We have just bought them new bloody beds!" I stuttered helplessly.

With a look that I have now come to know well, a kindly yet condescending one, as if addressing the village idiot, she explained the 'night time' sleeping arrangements. Eh?

Whilst I had a rather more erotic notion of what the night time arrangements might entail, her primary concern was that the cats would have full freedom of the house and that those who chose to sleep on our bed, may do so. My objection that Wacka alone was a dreadful snorer and one cat who I would hoy out in the middle of the night if he started his tractor impressions, fell on deaf ears. Fearing another rhetorical, I held up my hands in a placating manner and assured her that I was sure I could accommodate the new sleeping arrangements.

That first night, seven of the bastards slept on the bed. At least three of them were in between us, all 7 happily snoring and killing any chance of housewarming hanky-panky.

Looking back, I smile lovingly at the memory of the time when only seven of the passion killers shared my sheets. Since then, I think we have had up to sixteen in the bed at any one time. Several times over the years when I have retired for the night after Ali is already abed, I have seen my side of the bed covered in a thick rug of happily snoring fur, and surrendered. I simply grab a sleeping bag and spend the night on the sofa. On those occasions, I swear I can hear the assholes snickering behind my retreating back.

I'm sure there were other things involved in the new regime, dear reader. Things explained, rhetorical questions asked and 'looks' given to my wise-ass answers but I don't recall them all now. Suffice to say, it has been an education ever since but that was only day one and there was oh so much more to come.

Chapter 6 – We Can't Have Nice Things

Meet Chester. He is another puss who ended up with us after, in all likelihood, being dumped locally. He is a very affectionate big guy, who is still struggling to find his place in the household. He fails to understand that aggressive playfulness is not always the best way to make friends. He's fallen head over heels in love with our volunteer Becca.

Carpets, ah yes carpets. One of mankind's better inventions, I have always thought.

Picture the scene, dear reader. It's a cold, crisp, winter morning. The central heating has come on and pre-warmed the house for you. Feeling refreshed after a peaceful night's repose, you are gently awakened by the dulcet tones of a song bird upon your window sill, trilling a greeting to the new day. As you stretch your arms and swing your legs out of bed your feet encounter the deep shag of your luxurious Axminster. Your still sleep-befuddled mind strives to awaken, as those sumptuous woollen fibres work their magic on the pleasure centres on the soles of your extremities.

Yeah, well you can forget all that. A multi-cat household simply does not allow for carpets, rugs or any other floor covering that might give you an element of pleasure in life. "NO!" I hear you exclaim, "Surely the man exaggerates?" Indeed, the man does not exaggerate. Let me explain.

First off, we have plucking. Whether you have invested in a bargain basement cord or have splashed out on an antique silk Persian, it makes no difference. That beautiful, freshly hoovered weft you have achieved now has little 'pulls' all over it because your little house vandal can't distinguish between your beautiful floor tapestry and a tree when it comes to sharpening its claws.

Pfft...plucking it is just the tip of the iceberg.

We return once again to the disagreeable subject of the three 'P's.' That ghastly trio of ejected bodily fluids WILL pay a visit to your beloved carpet at some point. And, in all likelihood will make repeated visits. Of course, you won't give in straight away. With the spirit of the blitz, you will grab your bottle of Vanish (other cleaning products are available) and with a new kitchen sponge in hand, heartily scrub away at the debasement that has been thrust upon you. After the twentieth time, your resolve starts to flag and you wonder how your solid-coloured carpet now contains every colour on the cream spectrum from Chantilly Lace through to Swiss Coffee.

We haven't even mentioned the dreaded bum scoot which will change your lovely SCS (other furniture retailers are available) beauty into a Jackson Pollack, in a matter of seconds. So, that's a big no to carpets. Sorry, but that's just how it is.

But what about polished floorboards? Surely, they are like Teflon to the turd and tinkle and so on?

Well yes and no. But mostly no. Again, picture the scenario, dear reader.

You have just finished a chapter in a rather enjoyable book, you chastely kiss your significant other good night and flick off your bedside lamp preparing to drift off into a peaceful slumber. Meanwhile, Tiddles does what he does best and has a tiddle on your lovely polished solid wood lounge floor. Some 8 hours later you awaken, have your coffee, and catch up with Dan and Naga on the BBC sofa. That 'tiddle' has lain in an evil puddle of wickedness all night long, undisturbed, and happily eating away at your Ronseal Ultra Tough Super-Duper Hard-Wearing 1000 year, one-coat guarantee varnish (other equivalent products are....). Whilst the damage may not be evident straight away, believe me when I say its insidious acidity has gotten to work. Soon enough, you will see the tell-tale staining and eventually, if left untreated, destruction of the floor boards below.

When it comes to preventative measures relating to cat piss potency, I find a good rule of thumb is to recall the acid-like blood of the creatures in the Alien film. Then double whatever you were going to do before.

After years of torn up carpets, vainly varnished floors etc, we have found the best solution to be vinyl flooring. It's hardwearing, easy to clean and actually is remarkably comfortable to walk on if you get a good foam-backed one. It's not the seventies anymore, so you can even save yourself the stigma of referring to it as Lino.

Let's move onto the subject of how you may wish to adorn your windows in a multi-cat household, starting with curtains. Strangely enough, felines get quite a bad rap for being known to climb curtains but we haven't found this to be the case with ours. It has happened in our house but invariably it has been kittens who have been the culprits. Kittens, who haven't yet been outside and are experimenting with the wonderful built-in crampons they have been blessed with (murder mittens, toe daggers....). The length of the curtain however, does matter.

In our house, from curtain pole to floor is a ninety-inch drop. Indeed, once upon a time, each of our windows was festooned with a lovely full drop hanging. With some behavioural issue spraying these too quickly had to go. We now have seventy-two-inch drop curtains throughout our home and usually the worst clean-up you face is some dribbles on the bottom of a wall or on your skirting boards.

Blinds. *sucks teeth

Venetians are a definite no. If you don't have a mental image of your cat tangled amidst all those slats at the very mention of the word 'venetian,' then maybe you would be better off getting a guinea pig. The same logic for venetian blinds also applies to vertical blinds; way too many dangly, tangly bits that may hurt your cat or worse still damage your blinds. Yeah, you heard what order I said that in.

We have discovered that roller blinds are a happy compromise. Most of these can be cleaned and if any 'accidents' do happen they aren't too expensive to replace. For the same reason, roman blinds do the job just as well. That is if, by this stage, your cat hasn't bankrupted you and since you no longer have any money, you resort to hanging bin bags for a bit of privacy come night time.

Ornaments.

Now, I understand that we all have those little and large things we love to display; whether it be some gawdy gewgaw from a visit to a foreign clime or some beloved family heirloom handed down through the generations. Please understand though, at some point your cat will attempt to kill it.

Avoid lightweight items that can be easily pawed off a shelf, precious wooden items that can be chewed (yes really) and treasured fabric items that can be desecrated by your cat in any number of ways. Through a course of trial and error we have found heavy, bulky ornaments survive the test of time well, as do items that you can firmly stick down (blu-tack etc). If visitors to your house enquire why you have chosen to accessorise your home with several types of brick tell them it's modern art and to mind their own business.

Electrical Items.

Cats have long memories and can hold a grudge like you wouldn't believe. So much so, that cats 'inherit' a grudge and have no living memory of why the original grudge was instituted. This has never been truer than with the advent of flat-screen televisions.

Many of us grew up with a clicky remote to operate that hefty box in the corner of the room where Tiddles could oft be found fast asleep. It was a bed; a nice warm bed. This is a fact understood and accepted by cats and humanity alike. Flat-screens were introduced and cats have neither forgotten this, nor forgiven us.

Whether trying to defy physics or just to give you a heart attack, cats have still tried to clamber up onto this 2-inch-wide shelf of plastic and take a kip. This is never a success, nor is it good for anyone's health or blood pressure. Anchor that TV down! A wall mount works best. If that's not possible, try big blobs of blu-tack (or similar) to fix it in place. Take your chances if you will but if Tiddles brings your treasured TV crashing down in the middle of a deciding penalty shoot-out, you have no one to blame but yourself.

It is also wise to get into the habit of turning plugs off at the socket when they are not in use. This is not a fool-proof solution but does help mitigate against would-be disasters. You can only imagine my embarrassment after 'giving off' to a BT lady on the phone about our intermittent internet connection, whereupon an engineer arrived only to discover that the wires in the socket were semi-fused by cat piss. 'Cat shaming' at its worst, let me tell you.

Other areas of concern may be toasters and kettles. Once a toaster has been pissed in, the toast never tastes the same again. 'Tangy' describes it best.

Be aware also of any multi-plug adaptors and appliances close to, or on the floor. Often the only warning you receive of an attack on your electricals is a buzz followed by a bang and a flash resulting in you scuttling around in your underpants, looking for a torch that works, so that you can flip the trip switch back again. Clearly this will immediately trip again if the offending damaged item is still plugged in. It's easier to just go and spend the night in a tent with a candle and good book and look at it again in the morning.

And there you have it. You cannot have nice things. Well, you can but they need to be behind a foot of plexiglass. As before, the above is not an exhaustive list but will hopefully give you a heads-up as to what you can expect. I think I should mention though, when it comes to pissing, that this is a way your cat attempts to communicate with you. It could be a health or behavioural issue that needs addressing and not simply a wanton act of vandalism. There again, Tiddles might just be telling you that they don't like your taste in ornaments or home furnishings and enjoy the noise the fuse box makes when it pops.

Chapter 7 – Tc AKA 'The Guvnor'

*Tc (THE cat) …. The main man himself.

It would be remiss of me, in the telling of my story, not to devote at least one chapter to Tc, aka 'The Guvnor'. I also wish to engage in jiggy with my wife again in the not-too-distant future and that's directly related to the standard of the chapter on this fine specimen of feline-hood. And I quote: "I know you think you're a funny fuc*er but if you don't convey his majesty and dignity with the respect and reverence he is due, your hand will have to be your new best friend and you'll need to sleep with one eye open too pal. I'm deadly serious."

She watches way too much CSI, nothing would link her to my death, for this warning to be taken as anything less than a genuine threat to my imminent wellbeing and thus I have no intention of calling her bluff.

From our very first date, Ali waxed lyrical about her cat, Tc. He was her lifelong friend, with whom she had walked hand in paw, through many of life's trials and tribulations. He was her confidante, her muse, best friend, and soulmate. In reality, when I eventually met him, he was a grumpy, elderly black and white tomcat with bad breath and squinty eyes. To her though, he was her safe port in the storm of what we call life and who was I to say any different?

I recall an early conversation with Ali about the import of Tc and how nothing and nobody would ever come before him, his wants, wishes or desires. I remember feeling very bemused at this and arguing that, in time when she came to know and love me, that this seemingly intractable stance could be reversed. After all, 'he's just a cat.' Once again, dear reader, hindsight smiles down on me patronisingly at the stupidity of my male ego. In no circumstance is there, nor has there ever been, such a thing as 'just a cat.'

Obviously, some of the heft behind her words was filtering through my man brain and I resolved upon meeting this Obi Wan of the feline world to not only gain his approval but indeed win him over.

Again, my naivety of the cat psyche was abundantly clear since gaining a cat's approval is akin to seeking the same from a hard piece of stale cheese. In fact, the cautious cheddar is more likely to be responsive to bribery and cajoling and far less likely to shat in your favourite beanie. Once again, I know so much more now than I did then. Underestimating cats, in any shape or form, is a foolhardy exercise. I am now armed with the knowledge that we are only ever one genetic jump away from felines with opposable thumbs which would lead to us worshipping them as our cold and merciless overlords.

Regardless, I still tried my best to ingratiate myself to Ali's furry familiar. Despite ample time, I mostly failed.

When I first met him, chicken, and ham goodies notwithstanding, I got the distinct impression that I was being judged. Don't get me wrong, all cats judge. It's one of their primary attributes. However, with Tc it was more intense than that. I am aware that all animal lovers anthropomorphise to some extent but you will have to take my word for it. Tc looked in to my soul, weighed my worth as a companion and provider for his human charge and disdainfully found me lacking.

What resulted was, at best, a relationship based on a mutual love for Ali and an understanding that we had to coexist in the same home. That understanding decreed that he could do what he liked when he liked, have first dibs on Ali's time and attention, and if I wanted to spoon with someone at night, I should probably look elsewhere. Preferably in another bed. Preferably in another post code.

Still, I persisted. We managed a 'working' type relationship where he got the proverbial cream and I was left with the scraps. I'm not overly bitter, nor do I harbour much resentment about that time in my life. Ali was happy and I didn't have much going on anyway.

Whilst I never got to experience the bond with Tc that Ali had, one that only time and circumstance could have replicated, we did come to an understanding of sorts and I can honestly say he was a special little pussy cat. Despite being neither the biggest or toughest of our bunch, all the other cats did seem to have a grudging respect for him. On many occasions when there was a 'set-to' between two of his siblings, he would be straight into the middle of it to break it up. A very unusual characteristic for a cat, as they are usually on the perimeter of such things, egging on the combatants and tossing in the odd weapon to make things more interesting.

And so it was that Tc became, for want of a better description, the 'boss' of the house. The other cats deferred to him. Ali worshipped him. I was his whipping boy. In fact, I remember with great fondness this one little habit he had of sitting on my sleeping chest at 5am every morning. With breath more than a little halitosis-laden, he would growl in my face, demanding his breakfast. It was even more charming because I never made their breakfast, Ali did. I know the wee bastard was trying to assert some kind of dominance over me and taking full advantage of my drowsy, comatose state. Chances are he did it purely because he thought it was funny. Cats have a completely sick sense of humour.

In those early days, there were nine of us living under one roof with Poppy (more about her later) joining us shortly afterwards. Somehow, we all ticked along nicely, with only the odd bump in the road. We each had our place in the family unit, with Tc very much the patriarch. I was starting to experience a rare contentment with my life, that had thus far been elusive. It was around this time that we started to discuss the possibility of expanding our family further, establishing a more concrete arrangement for our kids. In the spirit of optimism, I gently put the feelers out to see whether the idea of marriage might be amenable and there was no one more surprised than me when I found that it was. On the proviso that the status quo we had would continue, Ali said yes when I asked her to marry me.

And married we got, with Tc at the heart of it.

Sadly, Tc passed away in the November of 2015, not long before his 18th birthday. He had been ill for a time preceding his passing, suffering from kidney disease.

Chapter 8 – No Sex Please.... We Have Cats

Meet Izzy.... As a borderline semi-feral, she is at her happiest when cuddled up with Darwin, which is most of the time. She forgets her shyness when the toys come out and can be loved and fussed but only when Darwin is in the immediate vicinity.

I hummed and hawed about writing this chapter. Firstly, because I come from an ultra-conservative background where sex was only ever talked about in hushed tones and usually in an explanatory, contextual type way, as in, "Mummy why does this doggy want a piggy back ride?" Secondly, I feel the whole subject of conjugal carnality is a very private matter, something which is the sole domain of the two committed, consenting adults who are involved. And obviously their cat(s). In addition, for the sake of the overall integrity of the book, this chapter was germane. And, more importantly, provided me with the chance to crack a few smutty gags. It was too good to pass up.

Realisation that any resident kitties could become a potential problem in the whole bedroom department initially dawned on me with the acquaintance of one Tc. I think, for the average couple, when the flames of ardour are well and truly alight, any furry little body who might be fast asleep in the intended place of passion (the bed, kitchen table, inside the wardrobe….) would usually receive short shrift and be unceremoniously shunted out of the way. This was not applicable to the venerable Tc.

By now, dear reader, you will be comprehending the magnitude of adversary I was dealing with in Tc. In all the beings I have ever known, whether skin or fur covered, Tc must be considered to be the most prescient. This was never more in evidence than when it was mummy and daddy's 'sexy time.'

No sooner had I excitedly untangled my boxers from around my ankles, sucked in my belly and prepared to do a full swan dive on my willing and dutifully resigned wife, than the wee bastard would appear. Remember that this boy had an exalted status in the house. He took precedence over EVERYTHING and man, did he know it.

He would never make some surreptitious, voyeuristic type entrance, rather he would announce his presence with a rambunctious "ROWARRRRR" and all jigginess would abruptly cease.

I pause my tale here to proffer another salient cat tip. This is squarely directed at any man wishing to embark on any kind of romantic entanglement with a crazy cat lady.

And it's this. Never, never, never come between a woman and her cat. You will ALWAYS lose. Look at it this way, an exhibition of self-control and patience will at least lead to some sex. This, my friends, is infinitely preferable to no sex whatsoever. Furthermore, it is infinitely preferable to being turfed out of the bed in the middle of the night, with the raging horn and at the same time patting down your pockets wondering where you left your car keys.

I digress. Back to that dear old endearing cock blocker of a cat, Tc.

Picture the scene. Me, laying in a distraught pile of unfulfilled sexual desire as Ali starts to coo over Tc. "Oh look, he just wants some attention. Do you think he knows?" My inner voice would be saying "He always wants bloody attention and of course he bloody knows. He was fast asleep 5 minutes ago." Outwardly, I would make non-committal noises of agreement and watched Ali nuzzle her favoured feline. Throughout this performance, Tc would throw me crafty glances as if to say "I'm freaking hilarious. She's mine ya little bitch and don't you forget it. Go have a cold shower, I may be some time."

Of course, there were times when the stars were in perfect alignment and the singular phenomenon of 'the woman being as keen as the guy' would occur. At these miraculous junctures, Tc would be gently, but firmly, placed on the bedside table. On these occasions, you could be forgiven for thinking I might enjoy some small sense of victory. But he would still have the last laugh by staring at me unnervingly pre, during and post coitus. It always felt like he was scrutinising my technique and would then bad mouth me to the rest of the cats.

Sadly, as you know the old boy has passed on to Rainbow Bridge. In a strange kind of way, I miss that little 'tug-of-war 'for Ali's affection. It was agreed from an incredibly early stage that Tc got all sorts of special dispensations and I suppose my 'making way' was just me honouring that agreement. Others, Poppy, and Banoo for example, have chanced their arm (paw) at disrupting nocturnal shenanigans but to no avail. So far. Yes, there will be times when 'on a promise' will be downgraded to a 'maybe but probably not' if certain kids get sick etc. However, to all intents and purposes, I now have fairly unimpeded access to my very own 'sex kitten.'

On reflection that last sentence may or may not make the final edit. If the kids ever got wind of it, I know for sure I have just 'jinxed' myself and will probably never have sex again.

Chapter 9 – What Do You Mean We Are Getting A Dog?

Meet Poppy (Popster, Poppylicious, Lish, Hoover, The Po-Po)

We have never hidden the fact that cats are our preferred love. However, as animal lovers, we have also happily thrown open our arms in welcoming other critters. The first of such critters is Poppy, the beautiful little doggy in the photo.

Poppy joined the crew in March of 2014, when we saw a local ad seeking a home for her. Her current owner's life circumstances had changed and she could no longer give her the adequate care she needed. We had previously discussed adding a dog to our family and felt that when the right one came along, we would know and as long as there were no cat related fisticuffs, he/she would be a welcome addition. Poppy came to our home for an 'interview' where she won both of us over instantly, leaving her previous owner satisfied that she was in capable, loving hands.

I'll not lie, when initial discussions about getting a dog arose, I had a mental image of some fearsome hound called Caligula or Brutus or some such warrior name, who would faithfully shadow my every step and be an instinctive furry vessel of loyalty and love. Especially since I wasn't receiving that from most of the cats, who barely tolerated me.

What we did get was a five-year-old Yorkshire Terrier called Poppy who immediately fell head over heels in love with Ali.

A man can't get a break in this house. You try being married to Dr freaking Dolittle.

Ali has often joked that I should get a tortoise and attach it to a brick that I could then take everywhere with me and it wouldn't be able to get away. What a ridiculous notion. I want love that is freely given, not physically bound to me in a twisted mockery of affection based on my location at any given time. I would call him Henry and we would be best friends forever. And maybe we could go on fun road trips together.

As it was, Poppy settled in very quickly. She got along well with the cats and gave us the added dimension of being able to take her out for walks. She never suffered the identity crisis of whether she too was actually a cat but it soon became apparent that she didn't consider herself to be a dog either. I'm still not sure whether she actually saw herself as another human per se but there was a definite dividing line between the cats and Poppy, Ali, and myself. This was never more evident than the handful of times we had to leave home without her and the dirty protest we returned to. Mind you, had I been left home alone with just the cats I may have done similarly.

Poppy gave a rounded and welcome aspect to our family as a whole. Not that the cats were lacking in any way but as dog lovers know, they offer a special kind of companionship and are far less likely to smother you with a pillow while you sleep. I say 'far less' because as with a lot of things in life, you can never discount something completely; even a canine murder attempt with a soft furnishing.

Like a lot of inexplicable things with animal behaviour,

we were both surprised and delighted when Tc handed over the mantle of 'peace-keeper' to Poppy. This earned her the moniker of 'The Po-Po'. Almost as soon as a kerfuffle would begin, Poppy would be in the middle of things quick as a shot, even going so far as to chase the aggressor from the room. A welcome pair of extra hands (paws) was very much appreciated by Ali and myself, even if it did reinforce the notion of 'them and us' that Poppy was clearly developing in her little mind.

At the same time as showing this perceptive intuition, Poppy does have a fairly wide dumb streak, bless her. For instance, having wolfed down her food at breakneck speed, she will share a perplexed look with us. She seems to wonder why the cats are eating at their leisure with bowls still mostly full, whilst even the pattern has been totally removed from hers. The look of hurt at the injustice of the universe in the whole "Why is just my bowl empty?" no longer tugs at our heart-strings, as guiltily refilling her bowl had her on her way to looking like a pot-bellied pig.

With Poppy having now come to an understanding of meal times and how much she is or is not allowed to eat, she has become like a devious a child secreting away all the strawberry cremes from a tin of Quality Street and hiding them under the pillow thinking you won't notice. Upon finishing her dinner, she will now zone in on any kibbles that fall OUTSIDE of any given cat's bowl, figuring that as long as her tongue isn't actually in their bowl, the errant morsels are fair game. Poppy has exploited this technicality for some time now and neither Ali nor I have the heart to close this particular 'loophole'. Besides, it saves on having to mop the floor afterwards.

On one occasion, however, Poppy's love affair with grub backfired on us when we had a creative idea for a fund-raiser for our ever-increasing vet bill. The idea was that we sold numbered tickets, one number would get drawn and the lucky winner would receive some grand prize. To give the whole thing an extra cat-theme, we chalked numbers in a grid on the tiles of our kitchen floor, placed a Dreamie on each number and then 'released the cats'. The whole premise being that the last Dreamie to be eaten, upon whichever last numbered tile square it sat, would be the winner. It was to be a completely random and unbiased prize draw. Well, that was the idea anyway. Upon opening the lounge door and releasing the hoard, Poppy slipped in too and hoovered the lot down in about twenty seconds, leaving the cats non-plussed as to why they had been shut out of the kitchen. Whilst technically the idea still panned out, it was anti-climactic because of its rapidity. More fool us that we didn't do a trial run but had decided to go 'live' with it to an eager online audience.

This coming summer our beautiful little Popilicious turns twelve. She has developed a heart murmur and a luxating patella. Not quite the energetic little girl we first had but still an integral part of our home, family, and hearts and perhaps most importantly of all the matriarch of TC's Forever Home.

Which you will learn all about shortly but not before I tell you of our wedding day.

Chapter 10 – The Wedding Day

***Our wedding day. Tc is the one on the left. And yes, I'm
clearly punching above my weight but Ali doesn't have the
best eye-sight and I'm sure as hell not going to tell her.***

The morning of August 18th 2015 dawned bright and
sunny. It was the tail end of a mini heatwave that had the good
grace to last for our special day. Friends and family had travelled
from far and wide to attend what we hoped would be a wedding
with a bit of a difference.

Obviously, being animal lovers and already having
accrued a small family of furries, we weren't suddenly going to
forget all about them and have a day purely dedicated to just
'hoomans.' With a fair amount of thought and pre-planning,
we had decided on a quick registry job followed by a party/
reception in our big garden at home where all the kids could be
fully involved in the celebratory nuptials. As it transpired, this
involved them being begrudgingly photographed ad infinitum
and a number of chicken thighs going missing from the
barbeque. But I get ahead of myself.

Ever with the no-nonsense approach, Ali woke early, fed the kids, cleaned the litter trays, and made the house presentable for our imminent guests. Before any female readers take offence and attempt to throw their burning bras at me decrying the fact that I would allow this to happen on her wedding day and that, 'of all days, couldn't I have pitched in,' I will say in my defence that she likes to do it 'properly.' This is something with which I only have a passing acquaintance. Besides, I wanted a lay in.

On awakening from a blissful and refreshing slumber myself, it didn't take me long to see that something was wrong. For the day to be 'complete and perfect,' indeed for the wedding to actually proceed at all, my wife-to-be required for all the kids to be present. This was a non-negotiable red line. And Darwin had gone missing. I have never been able to ascertain whether this intractable stance applied to my presence too.

Now, old Hairy Hole had, of late, gotten in touch with his inner hunter and had started to roam the local fields. He had single-handedly (pawdedly?) begun to decimate the local rabbit population. Think of Watership Down but with more blood and gore and the absence of Art Garfunkel's dulcet tones denoting some kind of happy conclusion. Now I'm thinking of General Woundwort, sleep won't come easy tonight.

We had previously gone searching for the big eejit after his previous jaunts had left him away from home too long. Through a process of elimination, we had found him at the home of Rosemary and Jay, now good friends, whose garden bordered a rabbit-rich, overgrown habitat about half a mile away from us. Added to this, Rosemary, a massive cat lover herself, may or may not have been feeding him salmon. Along with the suppositious salmon, there were more than likely other treats. In fact, I know there were. I'm looking at you Rosemary. A self-serving feline was quite literally never going to refuse extra treats, even if it meant assuaging his doting mother's angst on her wedding day.

Full on panic was averted after a phone call established

that Darwin was indeed with Rosemary and Jay. Although he was highly unlikely to come home of his own accord and quell Ali's pre-wedding jitters, a couple of friends assured us they would go fetch him. The process took longer than expected but Ali's prerequisite of full furry attendance was met and the wedding was able to proceed. Sue and Claire, I owe you for this still.

Not wishing to see my bride-to-be in her full glam before she walked towards me down the aisle in her full resplendent deliciousness, I left early with my best man for a cheeky Maccy D's breakfast to calm my nerves. I know its traditional for a groom to be craftily handed a flask of some hard liquor by his right-hand man, where a nip or two will staunch the flutteriest of nerves but I'm not traditional and find a bacon and egg McMuffin and hash brown do the job just as well.

The minutes crawled by and we engaged in small talk, like how the two of us could do a runner and be in Rio De Janeiro in less than 18 hours, complete with new identities. But who was I kidding? I had fallen well and truly in love with my crazy cat lady, had a full life mapped out for us, hopefully abundant in surprise and expectation. Besides my passport had expired the previous June.

I was repeatedly checking my watch. Finally, seeing the minute hand grind agonisingly slowly to the appointed hour, I announced it was time to leave the warm and welcoming environs Uncle Ronald provides and make the short drive to the registry office. I guess, like most grooms, that moment in time before the actual wedding is somewhat of a blur. This time spent welcoming the already arrived guests, a last check of your appearance, making sure your buttonhole hasn't wilted and hoping you don't have a sudden flare up of your unpredictable IBS. Before you know what's happening, the celebrant asks everyone to stand and the opening refrain of the bride's entrance song strikes up.

This part I do remember.

**

Ali looked neither left nor right, her eyes fixed on mine and never left them, not once. Those beautiful eyes that somehow, I had gotten used to but whose beauty I swore I would never take for granted again, were for me only. A nervous smile played about her lips. As she stood by me, I was blown away by how simply stunning she looked; the most beautiful bride I had ever seen, or indeed since. Yes, maybe there was a little too much bosom on show but it would have to have been a very generous dress indeed to accommodate both of the girls anyway. Any feelings of jitters or nerves fled, any harsh words that had previously crossed between us were forgotten and I was completely lost in the moment, lost in her eyes, and lost in the magic of our love. I even momentarily forgot the annoyance I feel at her when she makes me take my shoes off when I come in the house. I mean the cats can come and go as they please and they each have four feet! But, as I said under the influence of the plethora of endorphins my brain was bombarding me with, all such trifles were forgotten. After all we could revisit the shoe debate at a later time.

The vows went smoothly. Only when it came to her saying "I do", did my bottom do the old 50p, 20p for a few heart-stopping seconds. But then, we were pronounced man and wife. Life came back in to focus, the normal stream of time resumed and the ceremony proceeded.

Now, amidst preparations for the wedding day Ali had expressed the desire for Tc to actually 'give her away.' Despite being fully amenable to this suggestion, I did wonder about the coordination of this as well as the practicalities. I think in the back of my mind, I also had a small fear that Tc would deem me not good enough when it came down to the vital moment and I would be the first ever person to be jilted due to the fickle nature of a cat. As it was, the local authority had a pretty strict rule about animals on their premises so that eventuality never came to pass. A bullet dodged for me.

Understandably Ali was a little upset about this, so I prepared the following to allow the kids to share, at least in part, our special day.

Our good friend Bri, already prescient of the fact that Ali and I were in touching distance of barmy, stepped up to the plate and gamely read:

"As opposed to a traditional wedding reading, I would today like to share with you some heartfelt thoughts and messages from Mark and Ali's four legged and feathered family who are unable to attend due to Down District Councils policy on animals in council buildings. Incidentally, Ali and Mark believe this ruling to be unfair, especially as the cats feel that today should be all about them."

Firstly....

"Where have you gone? Why have you left me all alone? The cats have told me you're never coming back! If this is about the bedroom carpet, I'm really sorry... I have a nervous disposition and it was raining outside." ~ Poppy the dog.

"Really? You left me alone with the buffet? You know exactly what I am and what I am capable of." ~Benny

"Marriage is a solemn undertaking between a man, a woman, and her cat. As we travel this road of ups and downs and copious amounts of tuna, it is good to reflect on the true meaning of love. True love means that when two hoomans unite in wedded bliss that this in no way impacts whatsoever on 'THE cat.' I expect strokes, to be brushed, fed, and provided with a warm bed as per usual. If I choose to sleep down the centre of the matrimonial bed tonight, then take this as a sign of my blessing. I mean I may not...but I probably will." ~Tc

"As I watched Momma Al get ready for her special day this morning, I was taken aback by how absolutely beautiful she looked. Which

then got me thinking to how uniquely beautiful I am. Seriously I'm freaking gorgeous. Look out for me later, grease my good humour with some bar-b-q treats and I will let you take my picture. Obviously, you won't be in it, just me. You can then go to your respective homes and enjoy looking at me at your leisure." ~Darwin

It's testimony to our friends and family in attendance that barely a lid was batted but rather the read messages were received with warm smiles and laughter. I think this was mainly due to our guests being a combination of other potty animal lovers who completely understood the sentiment, and the rest of them who were either already aware, or had been warned in advance, of our eccentricities. Regardless, if ever we had a 'do-over,' I am confident we would do things exactly the same way with the added hijinks of actually sneaking one of the more biddable cats in and damn the consequences.

After the customary congratulations all round and obligatory photos, we got into our car as man and wife and led the procession home for booze and noms. No sooner had I put the key in the ignition than Ali started to seek reassurance that Darwin would indeed be fetched home for the day. Now I didn't exactly lie to my new bride but assured her Sue and Claire were on the case and yes, we would be graced with the big hairy hole's presence before too long. Extracting Darwin from our neighbours did take a little longer than any of us anticipated but he did eventually show up. Immediately, Ali grabbed him for a photo op and thus allayed any remaining misgivings.

As mentioned, the weather really was truly glorious and the rest of the day was filled with good cheer, good music, tasty food, and great company. After some initial nervousness at the sudden influx of 'hoomans' to their home, the kids too soon relaxed and joined in the festivities. Poppy had a day off from Weight Watchers and most of the kids just ambled around the big garden going from group to group to see what interesting titbits were on offer, who was willing to pet them, and who's lap was most comfy for a well-deserved snooze. To the delight of both guests and furries, my friend James, who was staffing the barbeque had quietly been getting hammered. With no one telling him to stop cooking, he had happily carried on producing hot food for hours on end until even our big boy Benny was replete. I would find half-eaten burgers throughout our property for weeks afterwards.

A bonfire was lit and coats were draped on shoulders as the evening chill set in. People talked and sang as dark fell, with the craic holding to a steady 90. Both exhausted and more than a little sozzled from the copious amounts of pink champagne Ali's mum had provided, we said our goodnights and made our way to bed. A perfect end to a perfect day.

It still grinds my gears though that they don't even attempt to wipe their paws as they come in...

Chapter 11 – Things That Go Squelch In The Night

Meet Angee (originally Willow). Don't for one minute be fooled by that sweet little face as this complete reprobate is a certified psychopath. She has moderate to severe Cerebellar Hypoplasia but that in no way impedes her quality of life or prevents her from doing what she wants, when she wants. Her trademark 'stomp' announces her wherever she goes and she has been known to catch us unawares by launching herself at our faces.

As cat lovers, it is very easy to think we have all the bases covered when it comes to the care of our animals i.e., food, warmth, veterinary expenses, possible assassination attempts etc. It is only when you have lived with a cat for a considerable amount of time that you truly come to understand the full horrors to which they will expose you. Perhaps none more so than what would have been, in your pre-cat days, the innocuous night time visit to the bathroom. Oh, how I long for those innocent, carefree days.

But those days have gone, dear reader, and will never return. Never. Ever.

As you will surely have come to know by now, beneath the surface of that cherished furry companion beats the heart of a stone-cold serial killer. A killer that has never been caught and summarily tried in a court of justice. Whilst you are happily in the land of nod, they are out there somewhere, decimating whole families, making widows and orphans, and at exactly the same time having just the best of fun. Think of Hannibal Lecter but without the sunny disposition. Obviously, we miss much of the actual carnage making but more often than not, we are left with... well with whatever's left.

It's at this point that I must digress and put paid to a popular myth about our beloved felines. No cat has EVER in the long history of cats anywhere, at any time, left a 'kill' as either a present or as token of affection.

Somehow this 'story' has done the rounds for years and, I can only surmise, been perpetuated by delusional owners who are completely blind to the true nature of cats. Therefore, these owners impute some kind of benign human attribute to their furkids, like kindness or gratitude. This is, of course, complete nonsense.

Let's look at the evidence. You may even be able to do this in the very literal sense if Tiddles has been out in the last hour or so. If, for some reason, you are presented with a complete carcass, it is because either your cat is full or it's laying down a warning. Maybe its saying, 'Look what I am capable of, human. Pull any more stunts like leaving me out in the rain again or serve me any more of that cheap own brand supermarket crap and I will not be held accountable for my actions. I know where you sleep.'

Or.

If the poor little critter on your door step is still alive, pitifully waving some mangled limb at you, then this is yet again your cat sending you a very pointed message. And this is not a message of an altruistic nature. 'Oh, look what I found in the garden Mummy. Can we nurse them back to health and try and find their family?' Bollocks. That cat knows full well what your reaction will be on seeing a half dead creature. They know that there is probably enough life left in the poor little thing for it to run up your trouser leg in one last pain-filled bid at refuge and freedom. Your resulting histrionics are merely cause for the cat's amusement and entertainment.

Then we come to the innards. That soft, squishy, glutinous nastiness that you can't quite identify but know for certain belongs INSIDE the animal. Once again, this is in no way an offering made in kindness or deference to their human masters as if they are merely our meek and humble servants. As if! The unholy mess presented to you is the bit of the kill that even the cat finds too disgusting to eat. The wee beggars only have one purpose for the presentation of these entrails. That, is to relish the look of disgust and horror registering on your face. Next time you're presented with this gory little spectacle try and get past your own revulsion and look at the cat's face. They will almost certainly be smirking.

My wife actually made a particularly good analogy about this. Imagine if a beloved family member brought you home say, the spleen or severed head of some poor, hapless victim they had just butchered. Would you squeal and clap your hands with childish delight whilst throwing your arms around them in gratitude? Or, would you slowly back in to a cupboard, lock it from the inside and quietly ring the police?

Exactly. Case closed. Let's not mention it again. Back to the topic at hand...

If, like me, the days of sleeping through a whole night without having the need to pee are but a fond and distant memory in the rear-view mirror of life, then you may well have to make one or perhaps multiple trips to the bathroom during the wee dark hours. In the zombified state of half sleep, when your internal satnav is only operating in safe mode, getting to the bathroom, and raising the toilet lid is a herculean task in itself. And that's in a normal house.

In a house overrun by cats, who will almost certainly not have the same nocturnal clock as you, this short and what should be innocuous journey becomes one fraught with danger and disgustingness. At whatever ungodly hour of the night or morning your treacherous bladder starts to sing the song of its people, which, despite your best befuddled efforts, is a song that will not be ignored, you will find the human brain is simply not designed to function at a level in-keeping with the aberrant obstacle course Tiddles has left for you to navigate.

Let's examine in a little more depth what hidden delights you may encounter underfoot.

Picture the scene. Having successfully navigated your darkened bedroom (turning on lights is just way too much effort even if it enters your head to do so) your leading foot encounters some form of unconscionable befoulment. What have you stepped in? What is the damage? Basically, what are we dealing with here? Following is a step-by-step guide to get you through this traumatic situation.

1. Don't panic! On one occasion, I stepped in something right by the toilet bowl and jerked up so quickly that I cracked my head on the shelf above. Even though I didn't actually pass out, it did leave me with a nasty gash. I explained it away by saying it happened during a knife fight with an intruder who I resolutely drove off. I wasn't going to say I had some unidentifiable

critters long intestine stuck to my foot.

2. Make your way slowly and carefully to the nearest light source. You may find, at this point, that you need to hop as a matter of necessity. Forget about your dignity because, if you're in this position at all, that ship has long ago sailed. No one is watching and there's no point in spreading that nastiness all over the floor.

3. Eliminate the obvious. A good rule of thumb is to rule out what we have previously referred to as the three P's. Piss, Poo, and Puke. These are fairly discernible by sight, smell, and texture. Or, to the perversely enquiring mind, taste. These can quickly be dispatched with toilet paper or baby wipes, depending on consistency of the P. Provided, of course, that your wife hasn't taken the wipes to remove make-up and failed to replace them atop the toilet cistern. In this case, you can file that little gem away for later to upbraid her about come morning. I digress.

4. Dealing with foreign bodies. So, it's clearly not one of the above and let's be honest, by this stage it's immaterial what it is, you just want it off your effing foot/feet. Intestinal detritus, you may find, gets entwined between your toes, and requires the shower head. Most rodent and bird internal organs can be dealt with, once again, by baby wipes. Frog guts, once again the shower. Rabbit remains may require a little more than simple, personal attention. Most likely, a dust pan/brush and mop/bucket will be required. There may be times when a full-on shower is unavoidable. In this instance, shower, get the coffee on, put your feet up in front of Netflix and watch one of your favourite films. It's best to simply write the night off as a bad job.

5. Probably the very worst-case scenario is that you have been left with some poor half-mangled creature that is still alive. The hour may not be germane for life and death decisions but you will have to make that

judgement call. If you think there is a chance of survival then, once again, your night's slumber is as good as over, because you need will need to source a shoe box with suitable bedding, whilst simultaneously finding somewhere to allow it to rest. This location will need to be beyond the accessibility of Tiddles, so that they cannot finish the gruesome job they started. The uber worst-case scenario is that you have a bewildered and angry half-mauled beastie, such as a rat or a seagull, backed in to a corner and seeing YOU as the cause of all its current woes. In this instance, emergency measures are required. Quietly back out of whatever room the creature(s) are in and shut the door. The next part is pivotal; stealthily sneak back in to bed without disturbing your partner and go back to sleep as if absolutely nothing untoward has happened. To continue the subterfuge, you have to make sure that upon awakening the next day, you theatrically throw your arms wide and declare to the world how you have had "simply had the best night's sleep ever." Yawning your satisfaction dramatically can only add to your Oscar-winning performance. Your 'piece de resistance' is to turn to your partner with feigned surprise. as if only just now noticing them, and ask with shocked sincerity "How on earth did you get those scratches on your face?"

6. You're welcome.
7. Prevention/ignorance is better than cure. Don't drink any coffee after 6pm. Fit a TENA bed sheet and just piss the bed. Face any nocturnal butchery by the dawn of a new day. It really is the lesser of two evils.

Whether you have one cat or, like us, a frickin' menacing gang, there is actually a mathematical formula to determine the likelihood of encountering something loathsome on this nightly walk of doom. Multiply the number of cats by those who are still capable of hunting. Then multiply again by those with incontinence issues. Then multiply AGAIN by those who would take some form of pleasure seeing you in considerable distress and discomfort.

That's right, if you own a cat(s) in any shape or form, you're pretty much screwed when it comes to 'running the gauntlet.'

Chapter 12 – TC's Forever Home

***Meet Sassy (Sassypants, Sasquatch)**

On the 1st September 2015, we officially opened the doors to TC's Forever Home. The aim was to provide a sanctuary/permanent abode for sick, elderly, and special needs cats. It was a concept with very definite parameters that had been in discussion for many months prior.

Looking back, the idea of starting our own rescue seemed a very natural evolution to the lives we were currently leading. Including Ali and myself, our family comprised 12 members and some of the 'kids' already fit the criteria mentioned above, many of them having had been 'rescued.'

I can happily, and proudly, say that the original idea was mine. Having lived with Ali for some time, I realised that what really made her happy and obviously gave her immense satisfaction, was caring for animals. Ali had had a complicated life in many ways and to see the joy she radiated in her role as a mother to our furries, in essence a simplistic pursuit, it didn't take much for me to join the dots and devise a possible life plan for the two of us. I had no idea whatsoever of the 'nuts and bolts' of what such a venture would include. Time and time again I have been blindsided by the sheer random events that have been thrown up by this life choice but at the time it seemed like a stellar plan. I still, mostly, believe in our mission, having walked this path for some six and half years.

Mostly.

As I mentioned previously, I only had the minimum amount of cat care experience at that point and Ali found me to be woefully lacking. So, I was happy for her to take the lead. Having already been a volunteer with a cat rescue for the previous three years, she had a long history of adopting waifs, strays, and cats that were oft overlooked. Her already accumulated knowledge was a great launchpad for what we were proposing to do. Besides, I reasoned that I was also one of those waifs and strays and she was looking after me pretty well. So, by appointing her as the boss, if anything went wrong, she could shoulder the blame.

First off, we had to establish a name for our sanctuary and the parameters of what kind of rescue we would want to operate. We also had to address the elephant in the room. Nobody would ever be good enough if we decided to go down the rehoming route. Seriously, Ali's standards are ridiculously high. Even now, if she leaves the house without me for some reason, she leaves one of the cats in charge. I just hate being told what to do by a cat.

Once again, the name was all me and one that I knew would win instant approval. As her beloved shadow and because of his patriarchal role within the family, Tc's name was perfect. It may or may not have also garnered me a whole host of brownie points which I may have traded on more than one occasion. With the rather simple consideration of the name, came the slightly more involved issue of what we would actually provide for our kitty clientele.

After much deliberation, we came up with the idea of a 'forever home.' Somewhere that a puss could live, never having to worry about the upheaval of moving or the possibility of having to adapt to a new family. Furthermore, we decided to make it more niche by extending that invitation to only cats that would struggle to find a home AT ALL in the big bad world. We came up with the term 'special needs' as a pre-requisite, an umbrella term that covered many different eventualities.

And there are MANY.

The overriding problem in animal rescue is that there are always more animals needing a loving home than there are loving homes offering one. This is particularly the case with cats. We reasoned that a 'normal' cat, one with no particularly bad behavioural issues, still youngish and with no major medical problems, would at least stand a chance of being rehomed. Sadly, a lot of people can be very fickle when it comes to homing a cat.

Rightly or wrongly, mostly wrongly, many people still maintain that a cat is some sort of accessory to the home. Something you just 'have,' like a piece of furniture or one of your other fixtures and fittings. The cat has its place and can keep that place. That is, unless it interferes with normal life or becomes a burden or hassle. I am in no way judging anyone, as this would have very much been my mindset once upon a time but feeling the way I do now, it saddens me that this rationale is still so prevalent in today's society.

Part of the explanation for this may lie in what 'worth' is put on a cat. For instance, many kittens and cats are given away free in local newspaper ads and on social media sites. This is, of course, an immediate devaluing of a living soul. The potential new owner may go as far as buying a bed and toys and setting aside a small budget for food. Some go even further. Responsible owners may also annually take their cat to their local vet for a health check, get it vaccinated and, if not already done, neutered. This is all well and good and to be commended. But it is by no means, not even close, to the totality of the proper care a cat needs.

Time and time again, we have seen the arch nemesis to a cat's comfort, wellbeing, and security. A new baby. The cat doesn't get along with the baby. We can't afford both. We can no longer give the cat the attention it needs. Suddenly Tiddles, hitherto comfortable with his place in the family home, has become a disposable commodity. Usually, after at least attempting to find a new home, the cat is surrendered to a rescue. Or, in the worst-case scenario, dumped somewhere. In the VERY worst-case scenario, put to sleep. What did poor Tiddles do to become such an inconvenience? How, all of a sudden, can his life mean so little? Probably not a comfortable passage to read but the above happens way more than you would believe and is still only the very tip of the iceberg of things that are decidedly UNCOMFORTABLE about animal rescue.

Another enemy of a cat's future surety, is if the cat becomes sick or ill. This may be due to perhaps a traffic accident or some unforeseen medical problem arising. Having done this now for a considerable time, I am still amazed at the variety of ailments I have now encountered that can affect them. New ones still come out of the blue. As a rule of thumb, think of all the many maladies and disorders that can affect humans and simply apply that to our feline friends. The difference being, that the large majority of us receive free health care and cats don't. And vets aren't cheap. When illness or injury occur, we return to the subject of how much people value their cat and its place within their homes. Depending on the medical condition, a vet bill can soon spiral from hundreds to thousands. Anyone who lives in a country where their medical aid is not free gets itemised billing. These people will testify to the price of professional consultations, scans, bloods, and a host of other things. Your scary looking vet bill isn't just down to a greedy vet. You are paying for expertise, time and much of the same machinery and apparatus that is used on humans. Machinery and apparatus that require a huge initial outlay and consequent maintenance and running costs. Sadly again, people who see their next holiday to Tenerife evaporating or the upgrade to their new car* in danger, Tiddles' immediate health becomes problematic. Rescue, dumping or a place willing to take a sick cat now become Tiddles' immediate future. OR, the needle.

Perhaps the hardest issue for people to deal with, is when Tiddles develops a behavioural issue. It may be a simple fix. Perhaps there is an easily identifiable medical issue or something as simple as you moving their favourite bed. Cats are sensitive creatures and even something apparently small to the human, can lead to the cat exhibiting some odd or destructive behaviour. It may, of course, be something much more complex. A solution may be difficult or even impossible to find. If that 'behavioural issue' involves pissing where it shouldn't, then it takes an incredibly special person indeed to take such a cat in to their homes. Rehoming cats due to behavioural issues is one of the most common problems we come across and one that is often exacerbated by turfing their Tiddles out of familiar environs.

I should interject at this point, lest some feel I am brushing society with too wide a stroke, that many, many, loving owners go above and beyond for the furry charges in their care. As far as some are concerned there isn't a single thing they WOULDN'T do for their beloved furries and have made many personal sacrifices to see that sentiment through. I salute each and every one of you. I would happily stick my neck out to say that you reading this now, the sort of person who would be drawn to a book like this, are probably one of those very people. Trouble is, by and large, we live in a material world where too much time and attention are given to the vain, transient and things with no real substance. Priorities are skewed and some, more important things, suffer as a consequence.

I fully understand too, that life can be very fluid. A person's circumstances can sometimes change overnight leaving good intentions and plans lying in tatters. Those plans may well have included the provision of lifelong care to your furry companion and you may genuinely find yourself unable to follow that plan through to completion. We have seen many such situations and our hearts genuinely go out to those people. If we haven't been able to help them directly, we have at least tried to point them to someone who could.

So, taking all of the above into consideration, we came to the conclusion that we would offer a home to the pussy cats that had literally no chance of being rehomed. At times, because of different circumstances, we have made exceptions to our original remit but for the best part have kept to our original mandate. Saying 'no' though is still hard, a mantra we have in rescue of 'you can't save them all' is sometimes the only solace you have to fall back on.

With the wedding out of the way (said in the nicest possible way) we opened the doors of TC's Forever Home on September 1st 2015 with Sassy.

The beautiful tortie cat pictured at the start of this chapter was known to us already. She was residing at a local rescue and had gained the label of 'problem cat.' Sassy would be a challenge and a perfect first resident for our wee sanctuary.

To start with she had a heart problem needing daily medication and this alone can be enough to put many people off. She was also suffering from a severe case of the grumps. Potential new 'owners' were met with a snarly, hissy madam who was in dire need of some social skills. Luckily for her, and ultimately us, Sassy was just one misunderstood puss.

Since Sassy was in the rescue where Ali had previously volunteered, we were fortunate to have some 'insider information' on her and witnessed another side to her altogether. Incidentally, this prompts another gleaned observation. Oftentimes, an animal you see while visiting a rescue is NOT a true reflection of their character or the way they may behave in your home.

Even the nicest of rescues, despite their best attempts for it to be otherwise, are high stress environments. This can be because of close proximity to other animals, noise, a steady influx of strange people and a lack of freedom or space. Think of your very own Tiddles at home right now, peacefully stretched out on the sofa with ready access to food and love. Then mentally transport them to the surroundings described above. Chances you are you would have one very unhappy pussy.

Sassy had been with the shelter for over a year and half and had become increasingly crotchety and frustrated. Unknown to her of course, this was scuppering her chances of being rehomed, especially in conjunction with her heart condition. Whenever Ali was on shift, she would let Sassy out of her pen. Sassy would run up and down the walkways and gratefully give Ali love and snuggles. Of course, Joe Public never got to see her like this. Knowing the cat Sassy was meant to be Ali was adamant about who would be our first TC's cat.

After a tentative meeting with the other kids that resulted in no major kerfuffle, Sassy explored her new home and, before we knew it, had settled right on in. In fact, Sassy settled so quickly, found her favourite sleeping spots, and joined the others for meals that after just 4 days with us, we were able to let her go outside. We still have the memory clear in our minds of Sassy simply running up and down the yard, purely for the sheer joy of it. Confirmation, if any were needed, that she was the right choice for us and us for her.

I feel I have to emphasise the point that in the normal course of events we would NEVER usually let a cat outside after only 4 days. The general rule of thumb used is a minimum of

2 weeks inside, before getting to venture outdoors. Every cat is different, as is every cat's introduction into the family. We made a judgement call with Sassy; one that proved right for her and us at the time.

Since Sassy first arrived, we have had over 50 cats come in to our care, some still with us and some not. Some have been complicated little critters, others a breeze. Sassy gets a special mention because she was our first official TC cat but every single cat that has come into our home has been special, some perhaps more 'special' than others....

The actual naming of your rescue, should you be insane enough to entertain such a notion, and 'getting' the cats, even with our strict criteria, is the very least of your worries. In fact, they aren't worries at all. The 'running' of a sanctuary is another thing altogether. To have at least some idea of what this entails, well you'll have to read on, won't you?

*NB the vast majority of people in rescue drive crappy cars, held together by rust and dreams and rarely, if ever, go on holiday. Most of us are fine (begrudgingly) with this state of affairs but would probably give one of our lungs for a week or two in the Mediterranean with someone at home doing the litter trays.

**At the time of going to print, Sassy is still with us, happy and in good health. In all probability she is presently curled up sleeping in one of her favourite places - in front of the cat flap in the bathroom. A furry door attendant refusing exit and entry to anyone she doesn't approve of. Which is all of them. I'd go move her but she'd only sneak back two minutes later.

Chapter 13 – Mummy & Daddy

Meet Pootle (Squishy, Squisheroo). Despite this wee madam being pedigree, a chocolate British Short-Hair, which are usually in demand, Pootle has quite a bad toileting problem so offers to rehome her were in short supply. Pootle had been kept in a kitten farm and made to have litter after litter, with not even a tray to go to toilet in (hence her problem). Smaller than your average cat she has proved to be incredibly resilient and when she chooses to allow you love her, loses herself in the snuggles. She's a tough cookie, who never backs down from any of the other cats and our home wouldn't be the same without her.

Ali and myself have opted for not having children. That is to say, human children - the little snot covered, two arms, two legs, variety. To say they are anathema to us is maybe a little strong but they are certainly up there along with things we consider undesirable, such as ticks, tape worms and fleas. If your child should happen to have ticks, tape worms or fleas, well that just adds weight to our already deeply entrenched psychological bias and is not really up for discussion here. Social Services may wish to have a wee chat with you though.

There are, of course, exceptions to the rule. We have some very close friends, and family who have chosen the path of human propagation and to these select individuals we have not only thrown open our arms, in embrace of their 'alternative' lifestyle but also in a more literal sense, the door to our home. Obviously though, the latter would require a prior written appointment. In addition, any visiting child should be supervised and kept on a lead at all times. Preferably muzzled and away from the furniture. In fact, it's probably best all round if you just leave them at home. I'm kidding. Mostly.

Rather than a malignant, deep-seated aversion to wanting progeny of our own, it's more likely that if we had children, we would probably feel the need to 'grow up.' Something which neither Ali or myself are prepared to do. Perhaps the only regret we have as a result of this decision, is that we both plan to age disgracefully and we will have no children of our own to traumatise in the process.

To truly understand how we adopted the monikers of 'Mummy and Daddy' you have to realise that we talk to our kids a lot. In fact, all of the time. Ali and Kaylen are merely labels that identify us to the outside world whereas 'Mummy and Daddy' denote the special relationship that exists between us and the cats. For example, "Mummy, has Moo been fed, she's staring at me again?" Or, in the third person, "Your Daddy is completely useless. Does he think the toilet roll changes itself?" As long as there is at least one square of toilet tissue left, that is ample for the next person's wipe. After all, I'm not Daddy Warbucks.

These honorific titles that have evolved in our home, help provide the kids with a feeling of security and an indication of their rightful places in this little ménage of ours. It signifies 'Mummy' as the primary care giver and eminent godlike figure and 'Daddy' as a general factotum and someone who can be leaned on for a sneaky piece of cheese.

Just the other day, I had a conversation with Ali as to when it was these homely titles first came in to usage. She seems to recall that sometime in the distant past, I was taking the wheelie bin down to the end of our long lane for collection when she hollered; 'Daddy you forgot to empty the kitchen bin!' That sounds about right. I seem to recall a flush of embarrassment as I looked furtively around to see if anyone had noticed. Thankfully, there were only a couple of cows in a nearby field at the time. Although, I am quite sure I heard them snigger.

Obviously, when something becomes common habitude, it's oh so easy to forget yourself. On several occasions now, in a crowded supermarket, we have addressed each other thusly. Any shoppers in close proximity look around nonplussed but probably dismiss it, figuring that our errant infants must be creating havoc in an adjacent aisle. Conversely, when we accidently let it slip in a crowded bar we just look like a couple of eccentric crackpots.

Though this harmless cognomen between Ali, me, and the cats may be considered a twee affectation betwixt a loving family, I do feel that, in many ways, it's no different than the usage in a conventional family unit. Just like 'hooman' parents, we provide love and care to our kids and meet all their daily practical needs, such as food and warmth. We nurse them when they are sick, remove dry poo that is stuck to their bum fur and regularly deep clean ears that are full of ick. Okay, maybe the analogy isn't perfect but you get the point.

Having read the above I just know that there will be many out there smiling fondly to themselves, identifying with the appellation of Mummy or Daddy. Like us, they know that the only true difference is that cats will never give you the reprieve of leaving home. Therefore, they remain a constant drain on your financial resources and energy until either you, or they, peg it.

So, there you have it. It is what it is. It's a little too late for us to start worrying about the label 'crazy' as that ship has long since sailed, been torpedoed by a German U-boat, and sunk to the bottom of the sea with no survivors. Besides, on the odd occasion when Ali does address me as Kaylen, my first impulse is to look around suspiciously thinking she has acquired a fancy man on the side. Who is this Kaylen of whom you speak? Is he better looking than me? Please don't leave me, I promise I'll change.

I suppose the one saving grace is that as responsible animal owners, all of our kids have been neutered, so we will never be in the position of addressing each other as 'Nana' and 'Gramps.' I mean that would just be plain weird.

Chapter 14 – Adapting Your House

*Meet Floyd (Floydy, Squishy) … This handsome boy came to us having been spotted dodging traffic in a local town. Attempts were made to find his owners but to no avail. Since he was semi-feral, although still young, we found a place for him with us. Another cat that loves love on his terms but he's awesome when he's in the mood for cuddles. Along with Pootle he is another we refer to as 'Squishy' because…well he's just so squishy. Not fat. Squishy.

You read it right, adapting your house. Did you honestly think that life could just carry on as normal? Oh, grasshopper you have much to learn, cats don't adapt to you, you adapt to THEM!

An early problem that arose at TC's was freedom of movement. This primarily concerned providing unimpeded access to the house from outdoors and vice versa. An initial issue was that the front door is PVC and reinforced with internal steel struts. Simply cutting a hole in it was neither a practical or cheap option. There is a secondary door behind the front door comprised of glass panels, way too convoluted and way too much hassle. So, what to do?

As I mentioned earlier, our house is rather old. So old, in fact, that when it was built, back doors hadn't yet been invented.

The house has since been retro-fitted with emergency escape windows but exiting the back of the house is still only possible with maximum loss of dignity followed by a minimal fall on to muddy ground. As luck would have it though the bathroom has a low(ish) sill and two small frosted panes of glass. I removed the bottom pane, replaced it with an equally sized bit of wood and inserted a cat flap in to that. A natty solution that worked well. Except, that is, when Sassy is fulfilling her duties as a bouncer.

Problem solved, right? Wrong.

Another issue with an old house, as I'm sure many of you can attest to, is the heating of it, not to mention heat retention. This is an almost futile task when your walls are solid stone. However, it is one you can at least attempt to deal with using certain mitigating measures. Measures that your average cat cares not one iota about supporting you with.

The first, and most obvious, thing to do, especially during winter months, is to keep all interconnecting doors shut to retain warmth in any given room. Our cottage is all on one level and we have some six doors which serve this purpose reasonably well. However, cats either fail to recognise the necessity of this activity or just don't care. In the early days, the cats were wont to paw open the door, all of which were left ajar, until it was fully open. Then, nine times out of ten, decided not to actually enter the room. The cat in question concluded that the room wasn't warm enough for a leisurely nap. Clearly the door that they had just left open and the incumbent effect of that open door did not register. This ongoing concern was only resolved by retrieving my trusty jigsaw and fitting cat flaps in to all of the internal doors. EVERY. SINGLE. ONE. OF. MY. LOVELY. DOORS.

With full and unimpeded access now sorted, we next turned our attention to the matter of beds. This is a complex subject. One that would have been preferable to approach having first secured a Masters in advanced mathematics. You can instantly dismiss, for instance, the equation of one cat requiring one bed. Nor for that matter one cat two beds etc. And this is where the maths gets tricky.

Most cats will have a favourite bed, or several favourite beds. These do not always include cat specific beds either but rather may comprise the sofa, your bed, kitchen table, the top of your head etc. The 'etc' is because the list is by no means exhaustive but very much exhausting.

Included in the mix is the 'time share.' Cats will randomly 'swap' beds throughout the day with seemingly no purpose or pattern. Believe me, I've tried to understand it. There is literally no rhyme or reason to it. Perhaps there is? I think maybe those experts who cracked the enigma machine in the second world war may have had a fair bash at it.

You also have to consider the 'temporary' bed. This could be a cardboard box; those are extremely popular. It could be your lap; wherever your lap may be. It could also be absolutely anywhere in the space-time continuum. Often the very place you are just about to step.

Considering that, at any one time, we have a minimum of 20 cats here at TC's, we have some 35 odd cat SPECIFIC beds. And we have the 'hooman' furniture. It more or less works, even if they do still manage to get in to the wardrobe and enjoy a kip on Ali's freshly laundered knickers.

Perhaps one of the most important considerations when adapting your house is the inclusion of scratching posts. Your future success in this aspiration may feel like emptying a bath with a colander whilst both taps are turned on full blast but hey, you give it a shot anyway kiddo. The cats WILL undoubtedly use them but only in addition to your beautiful Italian leather sofa, cherished walnut coffee table and stockinged legs. Not that I wear stockings mind you. Well, not every day.

Lastly, you must provide a constant source of food and water to satiate and hydrate all of your beloved furries. Some cats will wolf down food set before them at set meal times. Other cats prefer to graze at their leisure. Again, you must simply accept this as just another charming peccadillo of our favourite wee contrary bastards. I'm not saying that any of them would actually starve to death without unfettered access to food 24/7 but they certainly might act as if they would.

An added consideration, particularly in our household, is the aforementioned Poppy, aka the hoover. She will swiftly gobble down any unattended food stuffs or kibbles. Leaving food on the ground anywhere, is simply not an option for us. By way of compromise, we said goodbye to our dining table and that has become an ad hoc feeding station. I don't mind telling you this was done under a degree of sufferance on my behalf, especially because the cats are that much closer to ear height and hence more annoying when they start yapping for their grub. We were never much into hosting dinner parties anyway but the few times we have cleared the table for a meal with friends the cats take on a look of affront and spend the whole time trying to jump on to it. This tends to completely ruin any cosy ambience you have been trying to achieve.

By and large, water bowls aren't too much of a problem as the cats seem happy to share them. Just make sure you have plenty scattered about the house and you don't plonk them down next to a food bowl because cats don't like that. If your cats ignore the water bowls in your house altogether, don't take it personally. Yet another odd quirk to their deranged personalities is that many of them seem to get just as much enjoyment from slurping from a manky old watering can outside, seemingly oblivious to whatever gunge it may contain.

So, there you have it. Your house is basically no longer yours but rather a hotel catering for a bunch of ingrates. Consider yourself an indentured servant, who has been blessed to sacrifice your home comforts and that you are fortunate they haven't yet thought of charging you rent.

Chapter 15 – The Great Debate: Indoor v Outdoor Kitties

Pom Pom (Pom, Pompadon, Velvet-pants) This little beauty was bought to us by a couple of children who had found her underneath a bush in the local village. Once again, attempts made to find her owners came to a dead-end and being another semi-feral, we decided to take her in. Despite being neutered she is a shameless flirt with all the boys and can be found cuddled up with any number of them. Her name comes from when she was still a kitten and she had a wee fluffy head that perfectly resembled a Pom Pom.

Perhaps one of the most contentious issues among the cat community and one that people can be most vociferous about, is the contested issue of whether to keep your Tiddles as a solely indoor cat or to let them venture outside. I have personally witnessed heated online altercations on the subject that have denigrated to some nasty name calling and veiled threats. I kid you not, animal people are incredibly passionate about the 'rights and wrongs' of the care they give their furry family and can be incredibly intractable if you try and challenge them. Now when I see such an argument evolving, especially if it's flagging, I will happily throw a couple of verbal hand-grenades into the mix to 'spice things up.' Saying such things as, 'well it's only a cat' or, 'you can always get another one' usually feed the flames of conflict nicely.

The actual answer to this ongoing dispute is that there isn't really a definitive answer at all. With so many variables to consider, the eventual answer comes down to choice. This choice being made after weighing up all the pros and cons that your personal circumstances dictate.

For instance, those from the 'indoor camp' will forcibly argue that the outside world can be extremely dangerous for your little Tiddles and that the only true way to protect them is to keep them within the safe environs of the house. Of course, the threat of them being electrocuted after they have pissed on your Xbox is a negligible risk and perhaps a justifiable one too.

So, what really is all that dangerous about the outside world?

Well first and foremost is traffic, without doubt one of the biggest killers of cats. You cannot have failed to see, at one time or another, the distressing sight of some poor puss laying at the side of the road having had been struck by a vehicle. Sadly, these cats are nearly always dead, leaving some poor family none the wiser and broken hearted when they do find out.

Worse perhaps still, is when a cat survives a road traffic accident. Cats often get 'clipped' by vehicles, adrenalin enabling the cat to 'run on' for a bit. These cats often die later from their injuries or get discovered in need of urgent medical attention. In addition to the trauma and pain the cat suffers, these sorts of accidents also come with a hefty financial burden. Traffic accidents will often lead to the removal of tails and limbs and in some cases blindness or brain injuries. All of which are equally distressing for you and your cat.

Another argument used for keeping your Tiddles housebound is that surrounding predators that may be dangerous to them. Once again, we have to consider the variables. In this particular instance, geography is obviously a factor. For instance, if you live in the Americas, you could well have legitimate concerns about large wild cats, coyotes, snakes etc., depending in what area you live. I am not minimising these concerns, because of course many such creatures could do some considerable damage to your Tiddles and maybe even just make a light snack of them.

If, however like us, you live in the UK, the only prey animal you might have to worry about is maybe an angry badger that Tiddles may encounter while out on the nightly prowl. But it's more likely that neither creature will show much interest in the other. It's a bit of an urban myth too, that foxes pose a real threat to cats. Of course, there are always exceptions to the rule. Perhaps a fox may attack a young cat or maybe an extremely old one. Cats, for the most part, are just way too much trouble for a fox, what with all those teeth and claws etc. Foxes live mostly on small vermin and the occasional unguarded chicken. These are much easier prey for them and stand little chance of putting up significant resistance. This is a subject I have researched a LOT. The poor, already much maligned fox, often gets a bad rap and a lot of the time it's completely undeserved. In short, for your UK Tiddles, the most dangerous predator out at night is the cat itself.

There are other things that people may consider to be dangerous to their cats in addition to the above. For example, other cats, dogs, people, poisons etc. Again, this will vary according to where you live. You may live in a highly populated urban area with lots of traffic or, alternatively, dwell somewhere in the countryside that is sparsely populated. These are all important subjects for consideration when deciding what type of lifestyle you want for your Tiddles.

Perhaps the most important thing to factor in though, is the cat itself. Is it fit and able or does it have some form of impairment or disability? Is it old or still not much more than a kitten? Believe it or not, cats can learn, especially from negative experiences. This, in part, is why they are so good at holding grudges but it also helps them understand how the outside world works. Some even develop a basic road sense. Not ALL, by any means, but some.

Some cat owners wishing for the best of both worlds but not willing to commit to either, have come up with the happy medium of building a cat run or 'catio.' This is usually attached to the house in which they live. You have probably seen the online videos showing the time and expense cat lovers have gone to, in giving their felines the 'outside' experience. Beds, scoops, ramps, walkways, automatic feeders etc. Nothing is too much bother for their pampered puss. Some of the ones I have seen are so fancy I would happily live in them myself, providing my litter tray was emptied promptly, that is.

Ali and myself have taken the cat-by-cat approach, assessing each of our kids' needs and abilities. We have some severely disabled cats who only go outside under strict supervision as they are too vulnerable to be left unattended. This means that they can still enjoy a bit of fresh air and sunshine, albeit on a limited basis. I should add, that our two most disabled girls get some supplementary 'outside time' by means of a special kitty pram. This is now a popular feature on local walks and hardly anyone stops us these days to comment on our hairy baby.

For our other cats with sensory impairments, limited eyesight, hearing etc, we built an outside run to which they have full access. It's some 40 feet long, with walkways and perches from where they can haughtily look down on us. As we all know, this is one of a cat's favourite pastimes. Living in the country as we do, we are for the most part, happy for the remaining residents to come and go as they please, literally treating the house as a hotel. A hotel where they never settle their tab but are still happy to leave you a disparaging review on Trip Advisor.

This will always be a hot topic for cat owners and one which that will, no doubt, rumble on and on with no real resolution. Ultimately, it is a decision you will have to make on behalf of your Tiddles and live with the consequences either way. Just don't mess the cat about. Suddenly deciding you want to keep an outside cat in may cause you untold problems. The very least of those problems being the constant yowling at windows and doors right up to the cat developing some serious behavioural issues. Most common being a piss-fest of frustration and indignation.

We all want our cats to have full and fulfilling lives. As humans, we are beset with dangers and risks the moment we step out of our front door. But life is about quality, every bit as much as it is quantity. Weigh up all mitigating factors and make your decision not based solely on what is best for you but rather what is best for your Tiddles.

*By-the-bye, if at some point in the future you find yourself online having a heated argument with someone about this very subject and some wiseass is there, shit-stirring, there's a good chance it might be me. Please make sure you message me and say hi, we'll do coffee or something.

Chapter 16 – Someone Has To Pay For All Of This

Meet Beans (Beansie, da Beans) ...This little girl came to us as not much more than a kitten, when her family could no longer give her the care she needed. She has a very mild form of Cerebellar Hypoplasia which only really manifests itself in having a walk/run like a prancing pony. A wee bit of a loner from the other kids she is always up for some love with mum and dad. Oh, and she has a massive crush on Wacka.

Cats aren't cheap. Especially if you have a number of them and even more so if they have health issues. To believe that sharing your life with even just one cat will create minimal expense, since it can be fed on scraps, and then assuming it will live a long healthy life without need for veterinary intervention is, quite frankly, delusional.

Although Ali and I weren't unaware of the costs associated with running a sanctuary, any savings we had were quickly spent. Any items we possessed of any great worth were sold and put in the kitty fund. I am still not ready to talk about the guitar I had to say goodbye to.

You have to remember that in the early days of TC's Forever Home, the number of residents we had was still relatively small but already the connected costs were starting to stretch us. Before you can even think of dialling the vet's number, you have to cover all of your base costs, which alone are considerable.

Perhaps the first thing that comes to everybody's mind is food; a subject made more complicated by cats being completely fussy buggers with a palate ranging between that of a finicky toddler to one who will eat only food to the standard of a Michelin star chef. Your average cat will consume between 3-5 pouches of wet food a day. This is then supplemented by a quality dry food. Buying a huge bag of dry kibbles once in a blue moon will simply not do since a long-term diet of solely dry food is not good for their kidneys. In fact, a completely wet diet will do them no harm at all and in all probability is better for them.

So, a bit of maths then. Let's say on average a cat consumes 4 pouches of food a day. Seven days a week turns that into 28 pouches. Add that to the cost of the supplementary dry food and you are looking at a minimum of a tenner a week. That's £520 per year, per cat. And that's just the food.

Another essential, unless your Tiddles is an outside cat, is litter. Once again, this comes in a whole variety of types, each of varying quality and price. Just to be a bastard, your Tiddles may well choose the most expensive one on the market.

Of course, you want Tiddles to be happy and healthy, so this requires regular de-wormers and flea/tick treatments. The flea and tick treatments need to be done every month and the de-wormer once every three months. Each of these will set you back between £5 and £10 a pop. Ignore these treatments at your peril. You will either have a sick kitty, possibly needing vet treatment for worms, or a flea-infested house. Good luck in dealing with that!

Add in your annual vaccinations and boosters and you

have what we consider as our 'baseline' costs. With, at that time, some ten kitties, you can well understand the kind of expenses we were looking at, and indeed paying for, out of our ever-dwindling funds.

Now, I have always been a bit of a wheeler dealer. I have an eye for a bargain but perhaps more importantly, know how to turn a profit, even on seemingly mundane objects. I had long utilised online marketplaces and was a regular face at our local, thriving, car boot sale. Desperately needing a new stream of revenue, we turned our attention in earnest to 'making money' using these platforms. But where to get the stock?

In conjunction with opening TC's Forever Home, we also started an online presence, principally on Facebook and Instagram. We had soon gathered a hard-core following of friends and supporters who have travelled this journey with us, laughing at our kids' antics and commiserating with our losses. The 'TCs Army,' as we affectionately call them, have been our constant companions and always step up, especially in any emergent hour of need.

Neither of us are comfortable in simply asking for money, however much we needed it, but we both agreed that it would be appropriate to put a call out for any unwanted goods or items that people no longer had a need for. And how that call was met! From the very start, our supporters have all been superstars. They will either periodically drop stuff off at ours or I will go and collect items from them. Nicer items have been put on online auction sites and the more work-a-day things gave us ample stock to be able to do weekly or bi-weekly boot sales. This additional revenue stream has been a lifeline to us, enabling us to fund what we do and, over time, add to our crew.

Also, by thinking creatively but more importantly thinking smart, there are many ways to make savings and cut the costs. Keeping a basic supply of animal meds in the house has saved us numerous vet visits. Such things as eye drops, ear drops, Loxicom/Metacam for mild pain relief and a probiotic paste for treating dodgy stomachs. One of the upsides to being involved so intimately in cat care is that we have gained the knowledge and experience to be able to treat all sorts of minor aliments at source. As ever though, if in doubt, visit your vet.

Shopping smart is also essential. For example, don't automatically assume that your local supermarket will be the cheapest for food. There are many pet food wholesalers and online pet supplies who offer deals and discounts. Obviously, a bit of work is involved in this but your time is invariably rewarded. So too with litter, some brands command dreadful prices for something that basically your cat is going to crap in and then you will throw away. Having converted our kids to wood pellets which track very little too, we found a local wood yard that supplied it for us, cheaper than any pet shops. And, technically, it's a fuel so you only pay 5% VAT, instead of the 20% you have to pay in a shop.

To further supplement our ongoing costs, we have also done pub quizzes, held fetes and online raffles, and even managed to get personal sponsors for each of the kids. We have been happy to try any idea that could generate some income and we have tried to do it in ways that are not too onerous for those participating. Admittedly, even with the added help of all the above, there have still been really tough times financially. We have, on occasion, survived on cheese on toast or fish finger sandwiches for weeks on end. People who are serious about animal welfare happily make such sacrifices and will cut corners to get by. And get by we have.

We had found our groove, so to speak, and were just about keeping our heads above water. The kids, along with Ali and I, were doing okay. That was, until April 2017. Our little world, our splendid isolation in the country, with our furry family, was completely shattered.

I will tell you why later on.

Chapter 17 – Keeping The Peace

Meet Duchess (The Duchess de Floof)... At the time of writing, this beautiful girl is our newest arrival. She was no longer wanted by her original owner, after a collision with a bicycle left her with brain damage and near complete blindness. With these two rather nasty medical issues she has taken a while to settle in. She's nervous of us, nervous of her new brothers and sisters and nervous of her new surroundings. Patience and love though, are reaping dividends. Although still 'flighty' she likes to explore the house, will happily accept cuddles, and has developed a love for the brush. She has now taken up residence on Ali's favourite chair, I am fairly sure it is because it smells of my wife's bum.

One comment we hear regularly from visitors to the house is, "I can't believe they all get on so well!" As much as I would like to believe this was some happy happenstance, that couldn't actually be further from the truth.

Cats are divas. Cats are primadonnas and all cats have a sense of entitlement like you wouldn't believe. Put two divas in a room together, let alone 20 +, and sparks will fly. More accurately, fur will fly.

The first and most obvious thing to do is make sure YOUR CAT IS NEUTERED. Apart from the argument of there being too many kittens in the world already and the many, many health benefits of this procedure, neutering is the single best step to take to supress aggression, especially for male cats. Whether it's fighting over potential mates, establishing dominance, or defending territory, nothing short of a bucket of water will separate two tomcats in the middle of a full-on brawl. Worst case scenario being that one of them is killed. Yup, you read that right. I wouldn't have believed it either but sadly it happens all too often.

If a cat has had a long-time companion in the form of another cat, they will, in all probability have formed some kind of truce. If you're lucky they may have even bonded. Older cats too, those usually well in to their teens, are often more chilled and accepting of a new puss. For those cats, noms and naps are more important to them. Very few cats, however, upon meeting a newcomer, will throw their arms (or paws) around the new arrival in a warm, welcoming embrace. This interloper is a threat to everything your existing Tiddles believes to be theirs. That could be its food source, its beds, or its unfettered access to its hooman's time and attention. Handbags at dawn usually ensues.

Getting 20 odd cats to live in peace and harmony, well perhaps not peace and harmony but at least tolerance and mutual loathing, has been an arduous road that has been fraught with trauma. Spats/hissy fits, alliances made/broken, piss protests and bullying, are all things you have to deal with, often on a daily basis, until any current bickering is resolved. A resolution is seldom achieved overnight.

When you observe cats, you realise that even the sight of a strange cat can set off that deep growling in the back of their throats and a raising of their hackles. But this is by no means the only thing that is 'triggering.' Unlike the 'hooman', whose primary sense is sight, a cat has senses that could be considered equally as important, principally the sense of smell. Although this may be blatantly obvious to you, dear reader, it wasn't something we had considered when introducing a new cat in to our home. But it is certainly something that we noted over time and began to utilise in the integration of a new puss.

And it was utilised thusly....

Previously, any new resident was given a room to themselves to destress from their arrival and acclimatise to their new home, at least the part they had access to. However, we found that even after a good 24 hours there was still a lot of 'argy bargy' when they met the rest of the inhabitants. So, what to do?

I can't quite recall who came up with the original idea. Well, it was probably me. I mean, I'm the real brains behind the operation. However, we acquired a large dog cage, set it up in one of our communal areas and put the new puss in it. With a nice comfy bed, a litter tray and food and water, it is the equivalent of a little kitty hotel room, albeit a temporary one. Usually, once again for a period of some 24 hours, the new puss could get used to the rest of the gang and vice versa. Of course, there is the usual hissing and growling at this intruder but there is also a fair amount of 'sniffing' involved with no possibility of physical altercations.

When a relative calm has been restored and any ruffled feathers smoothed, we simply open the door to the cage. The newbie, after a tentative look and sniff around, will slowly venture out and explore the wider environs of the house with little to no reaction from the already established kids. Such a simple solution to a sticky problem! Yeah, I'm fairly sure it was my idea.

The trouble is, even with as much foresight as we are capable of, there is always the chance of a fresh brouhaha. Cats by nature are highly-strung and only ever a heartbeat away from turning into a bloodthirsty nutter. Feral cats, for instance, will only usually congregate in the wild out of necessity to share a food source, for warmth, or to plan bank heists etc. A multi-cat household is very much an 'unnatural' environment for them. The mutual understanding that they are all getting a pretty sweet deal is key to them consenting to it at all.

Regardless, health issues can make them play up, as can jockeying for their position in the home's hierarchy. Stand-offs can ensue when two cats want the same bed, same bowl of food or the same hooman lap. The scenarios and permutations that can lead to a dust-up are near endless, something you have to work at daily to keep on top of. Think of it as a shaky peace deal brokered by a number of nations who are hostile towards each other but the deal is occasionally violated by random acts of unprovoked violence. Usually something like a quick one-two bop or the guttural yowling which can be a signal of full-scale hostilities.

If, having tried to preside over a multi-cat household, it turns out not to be for you, don't consider it as a complete waste of your effort and time. You will undoubtedly have garnered considerable expertise in conflict resolution and shortly be head-hunted by the United Nations as international peacekeeper and asked to exhibit your acquired skills in a war zone.

Piece of cake in comparison.

Chapter 18 – Darwin.... The Toughest Cat In The World

Meet Darwin (Hairy Hole, the Big Man)

On the night of the 5th April 2017, Ali couldn't sleep. She can never really settle if, for some reason, one of the kids hasn't come home the prior evening. So, on this night, with sleep evading her, she decided to get up. Upon turning on the lounge light she was met with a sight straight out of a horror movie.

I still remember her dragging me out of bed and me, in my befuddled state of mind, trying to comprehend what exactly it was I was seeing in front of me. Darwin was laying on the sofa literally covered in blood. To my barely awake mind, it was something straight from a nightmare. He had some kind of horrendous head wound and blood seemed to be pouring out of it. He was making deeply distressing snuffling and bubbling noises and trying in vain to clean himself. How he managed to drag himself home that night, we will never know.

At times like this they say your fight or flight response kicks in. I think, looking back, that I went in to a type of shock, trying to assess the situation but at the same time with absolutely no clue as what to do next. Our initial thought was that he had been struck on the head by a car but survived that hit. Pulling ourselves together, we called the out of hours vet. Luck wasn't on our side right then, as the closest vet offering emergency treatment was some 35 miles away. A 35-mile trip we weren't sure Darwin had left in him.

You may recall that earlier I mentioned coming from an ultra-conservative, religious background. At the core of my very being is a strong moral compass. Adherence to rules and regulations, dotting i's and crossing t's, absolutely NEVER breaking the law are all values deeply ingrained. Yeah well, that all went out of the window that night.

Hurriedly throwing on some clothes and with Ali bundling Darwin up in a blanket, we got in the car and shot off into the night. One small blessing was that, due to the ungodly time, there was little to no traffic on the roads, I drove like Jenson Button (I'm not a huge fan of Lewis Hamilton) as Ali did her best to comfort Darwin, repeatedly telling him to 'hang on in there, big son.' The journey lasted for both forever and an instant. Countryside, towns, and villages passed in a blur and in short order we arrived at the awaiting vets.

I should add at this stage in the recounting of this tale, that at no point did I break any speed limits on that dreadful night. I drove both carefully, albeit hastily, when the laws pertaining to any given stretch of road allowed for it. (Cough, cough.)

The vet let us accompany Darwin into theatre while he attempted to staunch the worst of the blood flow and clean Darwin up. At the same time, he was trying to assess the extent of the injuries. He initially concurred that Darwin had probably been hit by a car and that the rest of the night would see if our big lad would survive or not. Delayed shock was still liable to lead to his demise, as much as the injuries he had received.

As Darwin was doped up on pain medication, there was little left for us to do for him but follow the vet's advice to go home and salvage what sleep we could. The vet told us he would call when he had some news. Obviously, sleep evaded both of us that night but we were able to offer some small consolation to each other, knowing we had done as much as we could. Darwin was, at least, in the best place possible to give him every chance to survive.

Be it human or animal, waiting for a call for a medical update (an update that may give you the news of life or death) is the very definition of torture. The time is indeterminable. No matter what you do, you cannot relax. You spend countless hours staring at your silent phone, part of you willing it to ring and another part not wanting to answer it if it does. I'm sure most of you can relate to this situation, it's simply horrid.

The next day, Ali was sat on the front step drinking coffee and I was doing likewise on the decking. I forget what we were in the middle of talking about, probably Darwin, when the phone went off in my hand. With Ali looking expectantly at me, I'll not lie, part of me wanted to throw the phone to her and run away. Of course, I didn't. Steeling myself, I took a deep breath and answered.

I honestly can't remember much of what he said, he used words and terms I wasn't familiar with but two distinct things shone through and registered in my brain. Firstly, and most importantly, Darwin was still alive, though not out of the woods. Secondly, and more alarmingly, he had not been hit by a car but rather been shot in the face with a shotgun. Read that again. Shot. In the face.

Now, cats get in to all sorts of scrapes, some nastier than others, but none really catch you completely unawares and fewer are what you would term deliberate. Luckily, it hadn't happened to us so far; the closest point of reference we had of anyone making a conscious effort to harm a cat being via poison. A heinous act in itself, horribly common, and incredibly painful for the cat, but nothing like this. You even hear the odd tale of idiots shooting at cats with air rifles, which can still do irreparable damage. This though, seemed like next level stuff.

Of course, after finishing the conversation, I had to relay all of this to Ali, who immediately broke down in tears, crying inconsolably over who could even think of doing such a thing to our big boy. Darwin is such a softie. A placid, gentle giant.

I just remember getting mad, really mad. So mad, that had the perpetrator presented themselves to me at that very moment, I'm not sure I could have been held responsible for my actions.

Having established that for now, at least, Darwin was comfortable and we would be able to visit him later when he had been transported to our regular vet, we turned our attention to ringing the police. Surprisingly, they were prompt to respond, incredibly sympathetic and willing to investigate within the scope of their abilities.

With the police looking into things and with enquiries of our own started, it was concluded that, in all likelihood, Darwin had been shot by illegal lampers. If you are not familiar with this term, it is a sport, hobby (neither of these words describe accurately this disgusting practice) where a couple of people with shotguns go out at night, shine torches hoping to catch the reflected light of an innocent animal's eyes, and then start blasting away. Their usual quarry are rabbits or foxes, with some farmers giving their permission to the 'hunters' to do this on their land, whilst other farmers do not consent to it at all, such as our neighbouring farmer in this instance, rendering the activity illegal.

In some respects, the consequent media attention Darwin received from local papers and even a feature on the local TV news, made the likelihood of the culprits being caught more remote. In our attempts to gain justice, we pushed the story as much as we could. I think we were trying to encourage someone to come forward who may at least know something, anything. A few names did filter through to us but without proof, these just led to dead ends. The only real lead we got was from a keen-eyed neighbour who had seen two men acting suspiciously on the night in question, driving an ATV up a long lane near us where they had no reason to be. Our neighbour even had the presence of mind to make a note of the number plate but to no avail. When we reported the number to the police, they informed us no such vehicle existed Apparently, fake plates are a common tool used by criminals to cover their nefarious activities such as lamping.

So, no one has ever been caught for what happened to our boy. But the upshot of the whole deal, the furore we created, was that our property and surrounding area became a strict 'off-limits' zone for anyone even thinking of picking up a gun. It has been that way for the last 5 years now and long may it continue.

This particular tale though, isn't about the bastards who committed this wicked crime but more about the horrendous ordeal our boy endured then, and since. Before moving on though, I want to address the issue of your cat's welfare and where you stand in the eyes of the law in such a circumstance.

By a cat's very nature, if you choose to let your cat outside that is, you cannot simply contain it. This is recognised in law and so Tiddles is given the status of having the 'right to roam.' Not a popular notion for some, who perhaps see cats as pests, but completely reasonable when considering their innate behaviour. Also of interest, although it sounds a little mercenary, is that Tiddles is your property and therefore anyone causing Tiddles harm, can be liable to charges of criminal damage. I appreciate this is cold comfort if someone has dared to hurt one of your babies but there is some small consolation in knowing that if an individual is PROVEN to have caused said harm, they are liable for any associated vet bills.

It is a far from perfect situation with animal abusers seldom brought before a court of law but it is something. Enough about that though, back to Darwin.

Our regular vet at the time was a fantastic man called Dan (more on vets later). He is incredibly knowledgeable and one of the top animal surgeons in Northern Ireland. Darwin literally could not have been in better hands. Having said that, we were still not really prepared for the sight that met us when we visited our big boy that first time. A bedraggled puss, still out of his head on pain medication, with fur matted with blood from the horrid gunshot entry wounds to his face.

Ali went in to full 'mama' mode, hugging him and whispering reassurances in his ear while Dan explained the extent of his injuries. It was suggested that at the time of being shot, Darwin may well have been carrying a dead rabbit in his mouth although this is just supposition. If this were the case, the rabbit may have taken part of the brunt of the force. Of course, these nasty cartridges disperse on impact, spraying lead shot here there and everywhere. In this instance in our poor cat's head.

The picture below is an x-ray taken at the time of the incident. The white bits in the left-hand corner are flattened lead shot. The shot itself fractured on his jaw, destroying most of the bone, taking out teeth on its way, with the remaining pellets sinking further into his head. Some of them remain to this day, far too dangerous

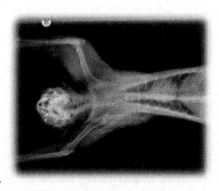

to remove safely.

What followed was a long, drawn-out, process of rehabilitation. One that has included numerous operations, considerable resented cage rest and a great deal of angst and stress for us all. Complications have led to yet more complications, which even led on one occasion to another midnight dash to the vets when Darwin had a bleed out. I get a headache even thinking about the journey we have had with our boy. He, for the most part, has been a complete trooper.

Amidst all the chaos we went through, came the mundane, yet inevitable, question of paying the treatment costs. And they were huge. To date, we have spent in the region of £10,000 nursing our boy back to health and the consequent operations he has needed for the gaping hole left inside his head. All of which was made possible by the incredible efforts and generosity of the TC's Army. These are people contributing to his care from all over the world, people never likely to meet Darwin but moved by the plight of an animal in dire need. The outpouring of love for him, either financially or in sentiment, left us truly, truly humbled.

Some five years later our big floof is still here, the only outward sign of his horrific injuries an Elvis like sneer. Inside ain't so pretty. Numerous skin grafts to patch up cavities have failed and Darwin is prone to infection after infection with gunky build ups of fluid needing drained. Oh, and he is one hell of a messy eater now, but I'm not going to hold that against him, am I?

In 2018 Darwin won a 'Bravest Rescue Cat' of the year award. We did tell him but he reacted with his usual equanimity, probably wondering what all the fuss was about. His hunting days are now over, whether his age or the incident is the cause of this we are not sure. He's happy now just to hang about the house or lounge in the yard when the weather is nice. As I sit here typing this, Darwin is fast asleep on one of the cat towers, in one of his favourite beds, basking in the warmth of the open fire. Do cats dream? I think so. He's probably dreaming right now about the time he came a poster boy for TC's Forever Home, albeit for all the wrong reasons. A time when his name was known all over the world, fame and adoration thrust on him. Adoration he was happy to bathe in. It will be either that or about chasing rabbits.

Chapter 19 - Why Exactly Do People Like Cats?

Meet Peanut (Peanutty, Nut Nut, Baby Boy) ... This handsome little devil came to us after he was involved in a car accident that left him with slight brain damage and near complete blindless. He's an absolute dote, with the disposition of a Teddy Bear. He has a loud miaow, which he often gets his bearings from and is one of the regulars demanding a time-share slot on his mum's lap of an evening.

Sir Terry Pratchett once wrote: **"If cats looked like frogs, we'd realise what nasty, cruel little bastards they are. Style. That's what people remember."**

I've mentioned that quote elsewhere in this book and I think there is a lot of truth in it. As a result, I have developed my own hypothesis on why it is that people actually do like cats.

Let's put a cat's personality and characteristics to one side for a moment and just dwell on what a cat looks like. Basically, what we have, is a panther that fits in your house. A panther that comes in a range of colours and patterns and is almost always soft to the touch and, let's be honest, is usually very pleasing to look at. In a world where image has become everything, cats totally tick all the boxes.

Certainly, growing up, many of us develop an awe and fascination for the 'big cat's,' the majesty of lions, the speed of cheetahs, the beauty of tigers, and the raw power of a jaguar. These magnificent creatures though, are admired from a distance, usually through the medium of TV. Very few of us are lucky enough to experience them 'up close and personal.' The domestic cat enables us to enjoy these attributes on a somewhat lesser scale. We get to have our very own miniature cousin to one of these glorious beasts, have the ability to pick it up, cuddle and snuggle it and to call it Mr Fluffybottom if we want to.

But are we really that shallow? Are we that transparent in our attempts to merely experience a 'brush' with the greatness that we witness in nature?

Well, yes. And no.

You have to remember that the domestic cat is only ever one generation away from the possibility of reverting back to being fully wild. Try blowing kisses on the belly of a feral and you can reflect on your naïve idiocy as they stitch you up in A&E.

We want the look and feel of the big cats but just a 'taste' of their true nature.

I would encourage you to read up on John Aspinall, a British philanthropist. He was definitely more than a bit eccentric but also a huge lover of the big cats. After a successful day at the horses, he actually opened a zoo aimed at protecting endangered big cats, with a focus on close interaction between the cats, the public and their keepers. Obviously, the man was sincere in his goals but money doesn't buy you sense. The death rate among his zoo keepers, because of his 'hands-on' approach, was horrendous.

So yes, cats are beautiful. A kitten's eyes will make your heart melt and you'd happily give a kidney for the privilege of one of your more recalcitrant moggies jumping on your lap for a spot of loving. And here is where, I believe, the whole philosophy of our fixation with cats, our willingness to open our hearts and homes to them, becomes a multi-layered issue. It far transcends their image and soothing tactility but encompasses the need for approval and perhaps is wrapped up in how we view ourselves, indeed, even how others see us.

There is an old adage that if you want a pet that is going to love you no matter what, then get a dog. It's an over-simplification of a relationship with man's best friend but broadly speaking it can be considered true. After all, I have never heard anyone refer to a cat as man's best friend.

From the day you get your Tiddles, you are on a journey of winning them over. You will strive to provide every comfort and luxury to this discerning feline, cajole and bribe it with treats. You will do all this in the hope that the bloody thing might grace your lap one day. There are absolutely no guarantees that this course of action will bear results. Cats have individual personalities very much like people and will react to your efforts on a cat-by-cat basis. Your endeavours may well be met with dividends of luffs and purrs or, just as likely, with disdain and derision at your pathetic attempts to curry its favour. There is no greater sense of betrayal than a cat you have showered with love, time, and money, grinning at you from the cosy environs of your neighbour's lounge window.

In addition to the constant fight for your cat's approval, are the often-rose-tinted glasses we adorn ourselves with, through which we see our adored felines. Our blinkered and myopic view of them is seldom accurate or true. When we say Tiddles is just a 'big softie who wouldn't hurt a fly,' he is in actuality a 6-kilo killing machine with the attitude of a stroppy teenager. He has been equipped with claws and teeth that are capable of rending, tearing and disembowelling but however much you protest his innocent nature, in the back of your mind you are fully aware that you are sharing your house with a blood-thirsty psychopath. A psychopath that may well enjoy a nap on a sunny window sill, or a munch on a craftily stolen piece of cheese, but a psychopath nonetheless.

And here is my next thought, are we actually jealous of Tiddles' true nature? Do we wish, perhaps, we were just a little bit more like Tiddles ourselves?

Possibly. Quite possibly.

Being part of the cat community has been a been a real insight for me as to the type of people who keep cats; their personality types and traits and their attitudes to their furry charges.

The 'cat community' of which I speak doesn't really include your average Joe who keeps a random moggy as a pet but rather refers to people who love cats, I mean GENUINELY love cats.

Within this community there are people like us, perhaps few and far between, but probably more of us than you may realise. People whose lives have been overrun by cats, pretty much to the exclusion of everything else. We are an odd bunch, slightly manic, definitely mentally unhinged, and long since given up the hope that we will regain a life of our own. Or, for that matter, ever regaining a peaceful night's sleep where your face doesn't get walked on at least once.

And then there are those who make up the rest of the community.

Being sensitive is almost certainly an attribute I would attach to them, as is being more introverted in nature. Neither is a flaw, rather just observations I have made. These wonderful souls, who make up the larger part of cat loving community are, to a fault, generous in the time, money, and attention, they shower on their pampered pussies. No sacrifice is too great, no expense is spared and no corners cut, not when it comes to their cat/cats. Some even imbue their kitties with an almost godlike status as the honoured guest in their homes at mealtimes and give of their everything in administering to their whims and wants. Of course, their cats just lap it all up, feeling this is only the standard of care they are entitled to anyway.

Here, I think, is the crux of the matter. Some, not all, people attempt to live their lives vicariously through their cats. The sheer juxtaposition of some cats and their owners is only really comparable to Mother Teresa being roommates with Hannibal Lecter. Two personalities the very antithesis of each other.

This seemingly contradictory imbalance in the relationship between the two parties, albeit an imbalance that somehow works, can be summed up by neatly parcelling a cat's main attribute in its entirety. In one simple sentence: 'They don't give a shit.'

Whereas, by and large, most people do.

I mean, how great would it be to sail through life with little-to-no self-awareness - if it feels good, just go ahead and do it. You would never have to worry about someone's perception or opinion of you, meaning that you could say and do what you like, when you like. A life bereft of personal angst, insecurities, or self-doubt. The wonderful freedom of never second-guessing yourself, every step you take assured and confident, puking wherever you damned well please. In short, the very life your cat leads each and every day.

Perhaps this chapter will turn out to be more controversial than I intended it to be. Perhaps you, the discerning reader, will think I am waffling psycho-babble and spouting shite. Perhaps some of you may begrudgingly agree. Perhaps I am including myself in my above cack-handed approach at psychological profiling. I know I would be a deal happier if I cared less for people's opinions of me. The mocking taunts of my fellow pupils when I forgot my PE kit one day and was made to do gym in my dirty y-fronts haunts me still. Had I been a cat I would have worn them like a boss.

Whether there is some deeper meaning to the relationship we have with our cats, one that runs deeper than their comely outward veneer, will, I think, largely remain a mystery. Perhaps the truth of which is only ever truly known to the two parties involved. Regardless, however much you like your cat, however much you believe you have a relationship with it built on love, respect, and affection, should you suddenly pass away in Tiddles' company, there is a very real chance he will be 'chowing down' on your fleshy parts before your body has even had the chance to cool.

Chapter 20 – My Heart Is No Longer Mine (Part I)

*Meet Betty (Betrum, Big Betty Bamalam)

Ever the pragmatic cat man, I am under no illusion, no illusion whatsoever, that the cats prefer Ali to me. Perhaps this is because I am wise to the constant shit they try and pull or maybe that I refuse to be at their constant beck and call. For instance....

As I explained earlier, we don't have a cat flap in the front door but instead have one at the back of the house, in the bathroom window. Of course, to our precious little babies, it's way too much effort to walk all the way there when here is a handy hooman to simply open the front door for them. Which, of course, they abuse ad infinitum throughout the day. Now I don't mind playing the part of the dutiful butler but if it just so happens, heaven forbid, I am bloody well doing something else, then I have no compunction whatsoever in making them wait. Not so Ali.

Any one of the given kids, at any time, simply must be let

in or out as and when they demand it. The hell they will! If they were going to be late for work, a work that helped pay their keep, I might be a little more prompt in getting off my ass. Chances are though, they simply want out into the yard to drink from a dirty drain or chase a leaf that's blowing in the wind. I have tried to explain to Ali that one of the very few virtues a cat has is patience. In fact, they are experts in it. I even pointed out that on one occasion Floyd sat patiently for a good five hours staring at a bloody drain pipe a mouse had disappeared up. But no, in, out, shake it all about. What the kids want, the kids get.

But I digress.

So yes, the kids like Ali more than me. To them, I am an inanimate object to be walked on and abused but who is still good for the occasional piece of cheese. My life in a nutshell - I am the human equivalent of an old chair who dispenses dairy goods.

And I'm completely fine with this state of our home's equilibrium, I really am.

But as ever in life, there are exceptions to the rule. In this instance of blatant furry favouritism, the first exception being the beautiful girl in the picture at the start of this chapter, my gorgeous Betty. Please stop looking at the picture now, she's mine and you can't have her.

The picture doesn't really do Betty justice. To start with she is a big girl, exceptionally large for a female. She's not fat, mind you, just well-proportioned and roundly curvaceous. Not fat. She is probably one of the most beautiful examples of a tortoiseshell you will ever see. Her stunning colours cover every hue of the autumnal spectrum, from browns and tans to dazzling oranges. She really is quite spectacular to behold. Seriously stop looking at her picture, she's not for sale. And not fat.

How and why Betty and myself bonded in the way we did,

is still somewhat of a mystery. But then, true love is a mystery, one that even the most eminent of poets have tried to explain and still fallen woefully short of describing accurately. You may as well try and describe the smell of the colour purple or how Gemma Collins became famous. We will simply never know.

I think with Betty, we need to go to the very start of her story and how she came to the attention of TC's Forever Home. And what a tumultuous beginning it was.

Betty had been surrendered to some good friends of ours at Almost Home NI, a local rescue, when her previous owner died. Betty soon established the reputation of being a little 'difficult.' I would not be stretching the bounds of truth to say she was considered batshit crazy and would take your face off as soon as look at you. I've always enjoyed a challenge.

Although we had been pre-warned about Betty's 'erratic' behaviour, it was only when we physically met her for the first time, that her truly monstrous psychopathy really became apparent. You may recall my observations of how cats in rescue centres often find them to be high-stress environs and this itself can lead the cat to behave in a way that it wouldn't in the normal course of events? I was certain this was true in Betty's case. Fairly certain anyway. She was definitely very 'bitey.'

For me though, the stars aligned, kismet was in the air, and I knew our paths were destined to be evermore entwined. Ali begrudgingly said 'yes' that we could have her. Whoop whoop!

I would be lying if I said that the transition from rescue pen to cat carrier was the very definition of zen itself. I would actually be telling great big whoppers if I said that. In actuality, what transpired was three of us in a battle of wills, for a good hour, hiding behind a dustbin lid in a fierce battle with a snarling, enraged beast, sustaining considerable injuries. But win we did and the now caged Betty growled angrily from the confines of her carrier, a low rumble that would accompany us the whole way home.

On reflection, I should have perhaps paid more attention to my surroundings, in particular the huge cheer that erupted when we left the rescue and the consequent fireworks that went off. Surely just a coincidence, it must have been someone's birthday or something. I wonder if there was cake?

On returning home we were a little flummoxed as to what sort of 'introduction' we would attempt. We hadn't yet introduced the dog-cage system and, going on her prior behaviour, we were a little hesitant to simply 'unleash' her on the rest of the kids. If my memory serves me correctly, we unbolted her carrier and legged it.

Providence was shining down upon us inasmuch as she warily crept out of the cage, sniffed at her surroundings curiously, all the while that deep growl at the back of her throat keeping any of our inquisitive kids well at bay. Nowhere near as bad as feared, considering if she had gone batty, I was quite prepared to move house and leave her to it.

Now, I can't exactly remember whether she joined the rest of the kids for dinner that night, mutual love of grub normally makes for a great bonding experience, but the possible nightmare scenarios of what 'could have' happened, completely failed to transpire. So, Ali and I just ignored her and left her to settle in however she saw fit. At this point, once again, I wish to divert from the narrative for just a moment.

Never, ever, force yourself upon a cat. At any given time, a cat is nothing less than a coiled spring. Any experienced cat owner can testify to this, how they can go from being fast asleep to having to unpluck them from your face in less than a nano second if spooked. You cannot bend or shape a cat in any way, by force of will alone. Their very being intrinsically rebels against such an approach. You let the cat feel its way, set its own boundaries, and you accept the lowering of its barriers as and when it's ready. Any other attempts at modifying their behaviour are doomed to failure.

Anyway, back to Betty...

After feeding the kids, we probably watched a bit of TV, generally wound down from the excitement of the day and started the bed-time routine. This usually consists of checking the litter trays, doing the head count, dishing out any meds, saying our goodnights and then lastly tucking ourselves in to bed. Which is usually around 8pm. Rock and Roll baby. In many ways a night like any other. But in one way a night like no other I have ever experienced before or since.

We all have our bedtime rituals, be it talking about the day, applying skin cream, reading, sobbing uncontrollably into your pillow etc. Once I had navigated the mysterious minefield of a womans body language, whether or not it was indicating that sex may be in the offing (it wasn't) I settled back to reading whatever book I was enjoying at the time. Any enjoyment was short-lived, let me tell you.

Reading in bed is a very personal thing. Finding a position that is both comfortable and relaxing is something that evolves over time. For each person, it's different. My favoured position, one developed over many years, is sitting semi-upright with my knees drawn up. They provide a satisfying book rest. Now, an unintentional tent-like shape forms beneath those knees. Just to be clear, it's a rough approximation of a tent shape, nothing contrived or planned just a happy consequence of positioning that occurs. It's certainly not a literal tent and it certainly doesn't have a neon sign advertising vacancies. Oh Kaylen, you poor sweet fool.

To you, dear reader, this may seem like a lot of extraneous bumf. I mean, who cares about the man's bloody night-time routine? Well please be assured I am merely painting a mental picture for you. This picture to give you a clear insight into the horror that was to follow.

This horror first came to my attention when I felt soft fur brushing the underside of my testicles. A fleeting, yet confused, glance at Ali confirmed my initial assessment that any conjugal fun was not on the cards as her head was happily buried in a book of her own. Bewildered and now starting to feel a little concerned, I slowly peeled the duvet cover back to have a peek. To my utter horror, Betty was happily nestling between my crown jewels. With rising panic, I carefully replaced the duvet. The dexterity, calmness, and precision with which I did so, would have had the world's leading brain surgeons smiling at me in approval.

I was now in the proverbial position of the man who has climbed on the back of a tiger, having enjoyed the ride but now having no idea how to get off.

Now the relationship a man has with his wrinklepurse is both intimate and sacrosanct. It is sensitive and it's quite important to us that they remain attached. The attachment status of my nads was now in serious jeopardy. Their integrity was, quite literally, hanging in the balance.

Moving only my eyeballs, I hissed at my oblivious wife: "Ali, whatever you do, don't move, Betty has fallen asleep next to my nuts."

I would love to say there had been an outpouring of love and concern from my significant other. I mean, I really would have love to say that. Rather, my earnest plea of fear and alarm was met with stifled giggles.

God, how I hated her in that moment.

You have to remember at this juncture, that the only point of reference we had for Betty was the demented head-case we had witnessed earlier that day. All signs pointed to an awfully bad prognosis, especially that is, for my happysack.

A hushed conversation that ensued established that there was literally nothing 'we' could do. Evidently, the best course of action was to keep as still as possible and 'wait her out.' A whispered conversation, I should add, held with the backdrop of the contented sounds of Betty now snoring in deep slumber.

And didn't she just stay the whole bloody night! A night for me which turned out to be the longest of my freaking life, not sleeping a wink. The only respite from my torture came when Betty decided to get up for a spot of breakfast.

Perhaps, with hindsight, that first horrific night was the start of the special bond between Betty and me. She became a project of sorts. I figured that whatever had happened in her life to make her so angry could be overcome with patience and love. A gripe Ali often has with me is that I often become focused on tasks and I miss the cues of when the kids need attention. Not so with Betty.

It took a long time and a lot of effort to temper the worst of Betty's behaviours. It has been a journey with many bites and scratches and with blood often drawn. But we never gave up. We both noticed a degree of mellowing, and this progress constantly spurred us on, cementing our theory that the path of patience and never replying to anger with anger was reaping rewards.

Betty, today, is a cat far removed from the enraged puss of old. She has come to love her love and only the unwary get the occasional nip. There's no real malice aforethought to it anymore. She will now regularly sleep with me or her mum with neither party losing a wink of sleep. If she lashes out every now and then because she's tired and cranky. But that's not really any different than most of us, is it?

As I write this she is tucking into a bite of late breakfast, still beautiful but age starting to show with the tell-tale signs of her backend starting to concave. It hurts my heart to see as I can't imagine our home without her, I want her to live forever.

So yes, rightly or wrongly, I have my favourites. I love all my kids but Betty has an indelible paw on my heart and I love her just that little bit more. It is said lightning never strikes in the same place twice but I'm not sure that's necessarily true. Within the ornery old heart of this pragmatic cat man is a place for yet another special furry but she too will get a chapter all of her own.

Not fat.

Chapter 21 – Your Vet

***The nightly conundrum of whether or not
there is room for us to go to bed***

Probably one of the more important chapters in the book covers a subject that needs due consideration and attention. Beyond our furries basic needs, their healthcare and general wellbeing should be your primary concern. A working, if possible friendly, relationship with your chosen vet is a must.

As previously discussed, the illnesses and ailments that affect cats are many and varied. Even having run our sanctuary for many years and witnessed first-hand the numerous medical disorders that can arise, we are still often blindsided by a hitherto unknown malady and the consequent corrective intervention that is needed to remedy it. Having a solid relationship with your vet at these times is essential in getting the best care for your cat and also in keeping you informed about what is going on. Not always easy with some of the medical terms that may be involved in describing in your cat's condition. But with an already established relationship, questions can be freely asked and answered with a certain 'dumbing down' of information if needed.

Hand on heart, and not wishing to curry favour if any of them happen to be reading this, Ali and I have been beyond fortunate in our choice of vets. Although it involved a fair bit in terms of a process of elimination, we consider that we have 'struck gold' not only once but indeed twice. Our former vets, Dan, Mike, Claire, and team at Flynn vets were superb in every aspect. Only distance, a 30 odd mile trip which isn't great in an emergency, forced our hand into switching to a newly opened local vet, a mere 5 miles away. For the last couple of years Catherine, Olivia, Grainne and co. at Donard Vets have once again surpassed our expectations in the lengths they have gone to in offering treatments to our kids. Treatments that, on several occasions, have made the difference between life and death.

The reason I mention both vets by name are twofold. Firstly, the care and attention from both has been excellent, and we, without a second thought, would recommend them as a 'go to' vet for anyone seeking professional and caring treatment for their animals. Secondly, and to the best of my knowledge, neither has ever charged us a premium for having to put up with my wise-cracks. Although Ali believes it is only a matter of time.

Finding a vet that is right for you and offers the best care for your cat isn't necessarily all about finding the first one in the phone book or even attending the one closest to you. There are several distinct factors you may wish to consider.

To start with, what type of vet are they? If you live in the countryside, the chances are that the nearest vet to you may specialise in larger animals, in particular the sort you find on farms. Of course, these vets will have a working and practical knowledge of how to treat your Tiddles but with a lot of their time spent on cows, horses, sheep etc, their approach may differ slightly. I am not, for one minute, saying they do not care but a lot of their professional life is spent working on animals that are considered as commodities. Tiddles however, is your life and soul and you want only the best of bedside manners for him. Some vets ONLY treat small animals.

Another consideration, and one that may take a little enquiry, is whether or not your chosen vet has a field of speciality. Obviously, all vets have attained the qualifications needed to professionally practice but some have gone on to specialise, or excel, in other areas too. I earlier mentioned Dan who proved vital in Darwin's rehabilitation. An excellent surgeon was needed for the type of delicate work our boy required and an excellent surgeon was what he got. Mike too, from Flynn's vets, a personal favourite of ours. In addition to his work with small animals, he specialised in the care and treatment of reptiles. Not particularly apt for us but illustrates the point of what specialised services are available out there.

Why people insist on bringing snakes and other nasty critters to this country I simply can't countenance. Perhaps I will author another book entitled: 'They should PAY YOU to visit Australia.'

A further issue is one of cost, and yes, it does pay to shop around. Whether its yearly vaccinations, blood screenings, scans, X-rays, and everything in-between, you will often note a difference in prices between practices. A lower vet bill though, doesn't equate to a lower standard of care. I should imagine some city vets for example have horrendous rental demands on them that the more remote vet doesn't. Each of them may have different staff requirements; machinery and apparatus to operate and service etc. Most of this cost, of course, filters down to you, the consumer. Whilst you will find that indeed many vets have a huge altruistic streak, a caring attitude being almost a pre-requisite for their chosen profession, they are not a charity. They are still a business. Sometimes a business that is in a competitive marketplace; certainly, one of the factors in the seeming disparity between what is charged for any given treatment.

My last observation, and one, I think to us, the most important, is that of personality.

Just as in normal, everyday life, there are those we gel with and those we don't. Be it colleagues, friends or family, personality often dictates the interpersonal relationships we develop with them. This can be a shallow, surface affair, or something a little deeper, a little more meaningful. You may think this is an odd thing to be talking about in relation to choosing a vet, especially as you expect that the vet is looking for a professional working relationship with you and not a new best friend. Of course, this is true, but there's more to it. Let me explain.

Very much like your family GP, your vet may well get to see you at either your absolute best or your very worst. It may be that you turn up at their practice in the middle of the night, barely awake, covered in blood and near to hysterics over some pet that has been involved in an accident and whose life is hanging in the balance. Conversely, you may feel you want to hug them in joy when said pet is bought back from the brink of death with a prognosis of a life of happiness and vitality still ahead of them. In the worst of scenarios, your vet may take on a role almost akin to that of a priest. That time when your beloved furry has reached the end of his life but may still may need that final assistance to cross over. All the above scenarios are extremes but can, and do, happen. All are made a deal easier if a comfortable, or even better, friendly relationship has been built beforehand.

As our family expanded, so too, inevitably, has our time spent at the vet. I'm not saying we have our own coffee mugs yet but we are certainly on first name terms with everyone and know where most of them like to holiday. From the girls in reception, to the nurses, and then the vets themselves, each of them has a friendly, welcoming rapport with us. Considering the heartache we have endured over the years, that very same rapport has alleviated much of the pain and anxiety we have often suffered.

I would be remiss if I didn't at least devote one paragraph in this chapter to the head honcho of our wonderful Donard Vets, Catherine. It's a testament to her professionalism, patience, and general kindness, that she treats Ali's neurotic worrying and my near-constant stupidity with the same long-suffering equanimity. She has gone above and beyond for us on many, many occasions and has proven to be a mine of invaluable information at the times we have simply needed to 'pick her brains.' A gem of a human being that has sadly been forced into a succession of human propagation; parental leave being the only safe haven away from our constant badgering.

I have long since lost count of how many children she has had. I think it's at least 12.

So, there you have it. Some of these things, you may already have considered, some you haven't. It's a decision that comes with a fair degree of import and one you are more than entitled to deliberate over. On finding a good vet, don't let them go and please be sure to let them know how great they are. Yes, they have chosen this career path but they are still people; people that is, who have to deal with the highs and lows of joy and grief, each and every day. Often switching betwixt the two in as little time as it takes for one appointment to end and another to start. I certainly know I couldn't do it.

*Girls...if you do want to get me my own mug, nothing too big please, I have a bladder the size of an acorn and don't want to be piddling all day. Oh, and a heaped spoon of coffee, three sugars and don't skimp on the milk. Ta.

Chapter 22 – Another Dog?

Meet Lemmy (Lembit, Lembit biscuit, Lemmy Kilmister)

Yeah yeah, I know this book is supposed to be about cats but take a look at that wee face and tell me you don't want to know at least a bit of how he fits in to our story. Go on, tell me. See, you can't.

Although adamant that Poppy was going to be the one and only dog here at TC's, things change. Life really should never be set in stone and when it boils down to it, we are suckers for a sad story. And Lemmy's was a sad story.

Our aforementioned friends at Almost Home NI, in addition to the incredible work they do in animal rescue, also provide a crematorium service for pets that have passed on. A service that we have availed of a little too often for our liking but a necessary one all the same.

I forget which one of our kids was due for cremation that day, but as usual we got all the latest craic with the owner, Karen and enjoyed a general catch-up and chit-chit. That may sound odd when you're taking a much-loved family member on such a sad and final journey but we were well acquainted with Karen by now. Her empathy and cheery spirit are often just the balm you need at such a time. Having made this trip several times, it has become somewhat of a formulaic routine. Occasionally, not always, this trip has included bringing home one of Karen's rescues.

Fully aware of what we do, Karen will invariably tell us of the latest 'problem' cases. Sometimes these cats have been suitable candidates for TC's and sometimes not. Another dog isn't usually even in the running for consideration. Literally NEVER up for consideration.

And then Lemmy was produced.

For reasons of confidentiality, I can't talk in detail about our little lad's previous life but suffice to say, he came to Karen's via animal welfare. This little puppy was thrust into my arms, matted, smelly and pathetic looking. He snuggled in closer for warmth and that was me done. Bearing in mind this was a situation we had found ourselves in before, some poor critter looking for a home, I turned to find Ali already sat in the car, arms crossed with a face on her. You know what face I mean. Can I get an amen brothers?

Refusing to look at me or Lemmy, he obviously wasn't yet named, she muttered something about needing to get home. Now, I can be a tenacious bastard when I want to be and just because I have a large streak of dumb running right through the centre of me doesn't mean I don't know Ali's switches and levers. With her still staring fixedly ahead, I softly opened the door and handed her Lemmy. Even as she made feeble protests of 'we aren't getting another dog' she stretched out her arms and embraced him to her bosom. And an ample, soothing bosom it is too.

As Lemmy buried himself into her chest, I still maintain

it only took about 3 seconds for her to fall in love with him and acquiesce to taking him home. But to assuage any damage to her pride, I will happily concede to her version that it was no less than 5.

Karen gave us a little more context to his life so far and we were completely surprised to learn that although he was such a little dog, he was, in fact, around 8 months old rather than the roughly 3 months we had guessed. Assuring Karen that we would facilitate any remaining vaccinations etc, we made our way home.

Names were discussed on the journey home, with Ali somehow thinking 'I owed her' and demanding we named him after one of her heroes, Lemmy Kilmister. She actually stated that if we didn't, he could very well go back to where he came from. She was, of course, bluffing. I knew it and she knew it but such are the little games that love is made from. I conceded gracefully and said that of course that should be his name. I politely allowed Ali a small smile of satisfaction at a mini battle won.

Arriving home, it was all hands on deck. With him being so tiny, we thought a bath in the kitchen sink would be germane to get rid of the kennel smell. So, whilst Ali made that ready, I attempted to calm down an apoplectic Poppy who was bouncing off the walls in excitement and distress. Throw a load of curious cats who were chancing their arms at an early bit of supper into the mix and you have just a small notion of the type of bedlam we were dealing with.

Having finished our ablution ministrations and dried him off, we sat back and admired our handiwork. Still shivering, with soulful watery brown eyes, he gazed back at us. Still in a state of obvious bewilderment and disorientation, he cut a tragic and pathetic little figure. Albeit one as cute as a button. Gathering him up in our arms we took him to bed.

Lemmy's transition into the family was remarkably

smooth with the only real issue being Poppy's reception of him. Many of the days and weeks that followed his arrival were spent reassuring Poppy that she was, and always would be, number one whilst showering both dogs with love and attention. Some obvious early jealousy was replaced with a kind of tolerance towards Lemmy; a tolerance that has continued to the present day. This is a tolerance that isn't averse that to having a wee cuddle and snuggling up together for a cosy nap. Poppy's seeming indifference though, is returned by Lemmy's enduring and unwavering adulation. Poppy is the boss and he's happy about that, happy to take his cues from her and to dutifully follow at her heels wherever she goes.

The cats' reaction was somewhat more of a mixed affair, however. Long accustomed to Poppy and understanding that she wasn't actually a cat, they still had a vague notion of what a dog is and how a dog behaves. They had never seen Poppy as a 'threat.' Indeed, Poppy had never given cause for them to see her that way. Consequently, they knew that a happy co-existence with a comfortable equilibrium was possible with a 'dog.' Lemmy, however, posed then something of a conundrum.

From the very start, Lemmy has had somewhat of an identity issue. He knows he doesn't belong as part of the holy trinity of Ali, me, and Poppy but he's not quite a cat either. Whatever passes for thought process in that little head of his though, is a mystery and apart from intrinsically knowing what 'walkies' means, he decided to throw his lot in with the cats. Who surprisingly, welcomed him.

At any given time, Lemmy can be found cuddled up to a cat. Full-on cuddles, mind you. It will almost always transpire that any heap of fur and hair will have Lemmy somewhere in it, with the possibility of absolutely any combination of the kids, all enjoying the ad-hoc pile-on and impromptu nap. Whilst Poppy may have been considered at least a potential threat, most of them well wary of the possibility of a snap should they piss her off, Lemmy doesn't even feature as a blip on their radar as being any sort of danger at all. Which of course is lovely but a little sad in itself.

What happens in the early weeks, months, and years of an animal's life, that formative period, can for good or bad, leave its mark. When the animal has had negative experiences in particular, the scars left may well last a lifetime. Whatever abuses Lemmy suffered as a puppy became evident in that he displays little self-worth. He is always the last to eat at meal times and we often have to encourage him to eat at all. He will instinctively cower whenever you call his name. Early on we knew that raised voices around him were a trigger that made him go and hide, although those voices were very seldom directed at him because he is such a well behaved a little doggy. Those who have rescue animals know that a lot of time is spent trying to undo the damage that has been inflicted on them by other humans. A situation that makes you both livid with anger while at the same time breaking your heart for the damage they have done to an innocent.

Many of us in rescue subsequently have little time for people at all because of this.

Should you visit us today, you will find a happy, bouncy little soul, who wants nothing more than to say hello and stick his not inconsiderably long tongue down the back of your throat. I'm not exaggerating, he gets right in there. Our more patient guests let him work away, of course recognising it as completely gross but at the same time knowing it makes him happy.

You have never really experienced a truly invasive feeling until our Lemmy has polished your tonsils.

Obviously with so many kids, doling out attention in an even and fair way is a constant work in progress. They all have their favourite ways to be cuddled and loved and all have their preferred forms of interaction. A couple of years ago we chanced on one that Lemmy just loves.

As the day winds down, goodnights are said and we go to bed, Lemmy will be there already. Patiently waiting, in expectation of HIS song.

Either Ali or myself will clear our throat, take a deep breath, and start with the opening refrain of: 'Ohhhhhhhhhhhhhhhhhhhhhhhhhh...'

The idea is that you start quietly, grow louder, and keep it going for as long as you have the breath to do so. Meanwhile Lemmy, fully cognisant of his part in this nonsense, flips on to his back with paws quivering excitedly.

Having reached a crescendo, and usually now red in the face, the song a-proper can begin. The refrain proceeds thusly....

'Ohhh... a belly rub'

'A belly rub'

'Everybody loves a belly rub'

'I said a belly rub'

'A belly rub'

'Everybody loves a belly rub'

Each time 'belly rub' is sung he gets his belly rubbed and the final line is delivered with raspberries blown on his belly. Knowing the song is now over, Lemmy completely loses his shit and bounces like an eejit all over the bed. This invariably has Ali and me in stitches and depending on our energy levels he may even get an encore or two with very much the same reaction.

The whole time Poppy looks at the three of us as if we have completely lost our minds.

*'The Belly Rub Song' is copyrighted 2022 with all rights reserved. If, however, Ed Sheeran or someone similar wished to do a collaboration, I am open to approach, get your people to talk

to mine.

Chapter 23 – CH

Meet the late, great Harry...(Harrybo). Harry was a massive black tom who suffered from CH. One of the most affectionate and soft furries we have ever had the pleasure of knowing. He loved everyone and everyone loved him. Taken from us way to soon when the coronavirus he was carrying turned in to FIP. He left a massive hole in our hearts that has never completely healed.

CH or Cerebellar Hypoplasia is a developmental condition in which the cerebellum of the brain fails to develop properly. The cerebellum is the portion of the brain that controls fine motor skills, balance, and coordination. The condition is not painful or contagious.

This hitherto unknown condition first came onto our radar with the arrival of one Miss Honey Beans. Having been forewarned of her condition, we immediately read up as best we could about it to familiarise ourselves with any potential problems that may arise and any provisions, if any, we may need to make to accommodate her. To say we worried over nothing, especially in Beans case, is an exaggeration but better to be prepared than found wanting.

Beans was considered to have a mild form of CH mostly evidenced by a walk mimicking that of a prancing pony. To a couple of 'CH noobs' though, we were still nervous, with many hearts in our mouth occasions. This happened particularly when she would jump on or off a surface of any great height. CH cats are indomitable of spirit no doubt but graceful they ain't. All four limbs seem to have a mind of their own, little coordination between any of them and the over/under judgements they make when leaping are enough to stop your heart. Once we realised that Beans wasn't in constant and imminent danger of breaking a leg we began to relax, she seemed happy and therefore, so were we.

CH is one of those odd conditions, a virus passed from mother to unborn kitten, one which manifests itself in just the most dreadful looking way but isn't anywhere as dire as it looks. The important thing being, as mentioned above, the cat is in no pain and I don't actually think the cat is aware there is anything different about him or her.

Upon seeing a CH kitty for the first time some people, and I suppose justifiably so, are horrified at what they are seeing. Whereas when time is spent with a CH cat, initial reactions are almost always revised, especially when you realise just how fab they are. A reaction that is not justifiable however is 'you should put it out of its misery' and this is neither acceptable nor welcome. And yes, some have reacted that way. Well, you're a miserable old boot Marjorie, how about we put you to sleep? Be careful what you say around a cat lover when you have limited knowledge on a given topic, even more so when you have little to no experience yourself about dealing with said topic.

And breathe.

So yes, Beans was our first 'taste' of a cat with CH and by

and large is an absolute joy and perfect addition to our already established clan. By a happy but strange quirk of fate, some year or two after Beans arrival, her older brother Harry (pictured at the head of this chapter) came to join us here at TC's. A true monster of a tom, who was also a CH kitty. But whereas Beans would be considered to be a mild case her big brother hovered somewhere between moderate to severe. Which in turn forced us to revisit our original research and make sure the house was suitable for his needs.

If you have never seen a CH cat, the best way to describe them is as they appear to be severely drunk. I'm not talking about a few swift ones after a hard day's work but instead someone who has gone a full-on bender and has taken to the dancefloor trying to keep up with everyone as they do the Time Warp. Hilarious, but prone to falling over a table and ending up with a broken leg in the emergency department.

A slight but constant wobble of the head is another tell-tale sign, as is taking a circuitous route when travelling from A to B, more often staggering sideways than forwards. A CH cat can achieve a fair turn of speed when it eventually gets going but it's the getting going part of the process it struggles with. The poor soul will often have a destination in mind but by the time it has all its limbs in order and pointing in the right direction it may well have forgotten what that is. I feel slightly bad in saying so, but it is very, very funny.

So, with our Harrybo showing all the signs of quite severe CH, we became far more alert to possible hazards and dangers around the house. You have to remember, that a cat with CH has literally no concept or self-awareness of their condition and behaves and acts very much like any other cat. And therein lies the problem. You cannot question the indomitable enthusiasm they have but a willing spirit and a body not necessarily made to match, can soon end in disaster. The biggest hazard in the house undoubtedly being high surfaces.

When a cat jumps down from a surface, be it high or low, they land with the grace and dignity of.... well, a cat. No so a CH baby. Nine times out of ten you are left with an ungainly splayed mess on the floor with the unfortunately too common 'clunk' as their skull bounces off the ground. It's sickening sound and one to be avoided if at all possible but one which will not deter the kitty from doing the exact same thing again five minutes later.

A severe CH kitty, because of their impairment, simply does not have the ability to jump as high as say, kitchen work surfaces but will happily pull themselves up on to a kitchen chair and from there to the kitchen table. Which they will then attempt to take the short-cut off. It soon became a matter of routine to tuck all chairs tightly under the table and to remove any sources around the house that be considered a 'launch-pad' to somewhere higher.

It was a work in progress but one which we eventually conquered after more than a few scares and after addressing Harry's determination to give us both heart attacks. The 'risks' of descending from the sofa and bed became negligible as they weren't too high and Harry had managed to develop a kind of flop type roll that only resulted in a minor damage to his dignity.

When you have a cat with a disability, even if they aren't aware of it, you still appreciate that there are aspects they miss out on which the 'normal' cats engage in as a matter of course. In particular, enjoying the great outdoors. I mean Harry did go out but it was always under strict supervision and he could only ever look on wistfully as his siblings climbed trees and scampered about the fields that surround our house. We did, at least in part, seek to address this.

One of our wonderful supporters (*waves at Ann) bought us a special 'kitty carrier.' I can dress it up as much as I like with all the fancy names under the sun but it was, in essence, a pram for a cat. A new low for my cool reputation (only kidding, I've never been cool) but a new high for Harry. A new aspect to Harry's life which he took to with pleasure and enjoyment immediately. It made for some interesting conversations with strangers when taking him out for a stroll but he was happy, so that was all that mattered. Besides, if they had shown us only a passing interest and left with the impression that we somehow just had a very hairy baby, I wasn't going to go out of my way to set them straight.

On one occasion we took Harry, stroller, and all, to a special cat fete in aid of another cat rescue. I have already described to you the 'calibre' of crazy cat folk and this hall was full to the brim with them. You will have to take my word when I say that dandering around the various bric-a-brac tables and raffle stalls, hood down and Harry curiously taking in the sights and sounds, people stopping us to coo over him, was not the oddest thing there. 'We' truly are a queer breed.

Harry was a complete pleasure to share our life with. One of the most loving cats ever to grace our home and taken from us too, too soon. It's one of few deaths we have had here at TC's that I have still not come to terms with and maybe never will.

Our beautiful big boy's legacy was more than that of happy and fond memories. More importantly it gave us knowledge and experience for what was to come after. And what came after was an angel in disguise in the form of a 3-month-old kitten we ended up calling Maisie.

Little Miss Maisie Moo Bobble-Head to be precise.

Now, once in a while, if you are extremely lucky, along comes such a pure wee soul that you have to pinch yourself to believe it to be feline. But Maisie is very much a cat and one who has been nothing but a source of joy and happiness to us. Again, she is diagnosed moderate to severe CH, but rather than having a bombastic approach to life she is gentle and cautious, albeit in a very wobbly sort of way.

Maisie was a first inasmuch as she was a kitten, Beans

and Harry being somewhat older when they came to us. Her condition was exacerbated at first by the general clumsiness of kittenhood combined with being CH. She soon navigated the house though, and worked out which obstacles could be traversed and which were beyond her capabilities and therefore, to be avoided. She developed an almost graceful gait, light on her paws and walked from room to room softly, almost as if on her tiptoes.

Like many of the other kids, she soon formed a deep bond with Ali, seeking out her lap and often happy to be carried around the house in a papoose type of affair while Ali does the housework. So gentle is her demeanour that Maisie has probably become our most well-travelled cat. If it's not too cold she will accompany the dogs on their walk, just content to soak up the smells and sounds. She has no concerns about popping out to the shops with mum and has become a regular feature at the boot sales where she is both adored and made a fuss over.

It says something when your cat has a better social life than you.

Although, invariably, Maisie prefers her mum's lap to mine, we have developed a lovely little routine come dinnertime and it's just between her and me. Being the smart little cookie she is, she soon cottoned on that mum was a vegetarian and looking for tasty titbits come meal time was a largely thankless task. Turning to her still meat-loving dad though, was a different matter altogether.

Right from the very beginning, we realised that to be able to enjoy our dinner mostly unmolested, we had to feed the kids first. We have done this faithfully now for years with only the greedy gorbs chancing their paws by attempting to get a 'second-helping.' I can happily ignore the little upturned faces gazing at me in expectation, knowing full well that they have already eaten and that should the situation be reversed, there is absolutely no way they would so much as even let me sniff their chicken wrap. My resolve, however, is not so staunch when it comes to Maisie.

With the kids fed around 5.30 each evening, we get to sit and enjoy ours around 6 pm. As soon as my bum touches leather, the soft pitter-patter which precludes Maisie's entrance, can be heard making its way from the kitchen to my side, where she then sits and looks at me patiently. With eyes that are seemingly over-big for her face, she gives me a 'look' that I am powerless to ignore. I then dutifully share my dinner.

Yes, I know this is a relationship built on her greed and my need for acceptance and love but like I have already said, cats are fickle creatures and I will feast on any scraps of affection I can get. Besides, it's not always a 'done deal' for Maisie as there are times when what I'm eating may not be suitable for a small pussy cat, if for example it contains garlic etc. At these times she still just sits there, looking at me, but now with a gaze of hurt, betrayal, and disappointment. And that I can't ignore. Every mouthful becomes laced with guilt and every swallow contains the bitter taste of shame. Many a meal has been ruined by my complete inability to ignore the silent pleas of a very small cat.

So yes, our little Maisie-Moo is a blessing to our home and a welcome addition to our family. When we were offered another CH kitten some 6 months later, a kitten whose existing family environment had not proved ideal for her, we jumped at the chance.

Enter stage left, Willow. A pre-determined name choice of ours that fitted as well as asking Vladimir Putin if he was free this Christmas and if not, would be happy to play the part of Father Christmas in your local shopping centre. A name that lasted about as long as most people need to have a nice bath.

Enter stage left, Angee. Whereas Maisie was the very epitome of sweetness and light, Angee (as she is now called) was her direct counterpoint. A complete thug who stomps around the house like she owns it, independent and forthright, a rebel without a clue. Intimidated by nothing and no-one, shyness considered a word reserved for wimps and no prey safe from claw or tooth be it your feet or face.

Getting the picture?

Being a grey she is undoubtedly a pretty cat but any semblance of delicate femininity ends there. The fact she was a complete nutter initially took a back seat to the more alarming issue of her 'poo problem.' Oh, dear God and all that is considered holy, her poo problem. A disturbing, buried memory that has only now been unearthed due to writing about this hooligan's part in our story.

I have not yet mentioned CH kitties and their, at times, 'complicated' toileting issues. Nothing whatsoever to worry about in regards to their actual plumbing but more of a... um... positioning issue. Some of these little wonders find it hard to stand still for any length of time, the length of time for instance, it might take to have a poo and so each develop their own unique positions in the litter tray where they are comfortable. Not a problem in itself and you certainly wouldn't want anyone telling you the proper way of conducting your bowel movements. The real problem is when a fresh deposit has been made and a case of the wobbles ends up with them falling in it.

The fervent prayer of any CH parent is that the embodiment of horror, diarrhoea, doesn't come calling.

Unfortunately, with Angee not only did it come a calling but unpacked its bags and said it was staying for the next couple of months and had brought its summer clothes just in case.

It was the fecking longest bout of an upset stomach we have ever known. So much so, the local chemist refused us any more sales of baby wipes as 'they were for the rest of the community as well.' A little ungrateful as our previous purchases of wipes had surely paid for at least one of their kid's university educations.

To counter this thrice daily faecal nightmare of doom, we developed a sort of 'poo watch' which consisted of one of us, having seen Angee enter a litter tray, shouted shrilly to the other for tactical support. Support needed, because although she could be bloody well coated in crap, she resented having it removed or getting cleaned up. Our response time became excellent, as did the clean-up operation but there were still the times we were either not present or got caught napping. If there had been a 'pinball' effect on those occasions the clean-up operation became more involved.

Ah yes, the pinball effect.

As I mentioned earlier, once a CH cat builds up a full head of steam, it can achieve quite a turn of speed, seldom though is it in a straight line. That's where the pinball effect happens. They career randomly and indiscriminately into inanimate objects which they, in turn, bounce off in their haphazard flight. Now imagine that with a cat covered in shit that is trying to escape your grasping fingers. Thunk...splat...thunk...splat...etc etc. I apologise for the distressing images this may have forced you to conjure up. Actually, I don't, you never had to clean up the ungodly mess.

I think though, by far, the worst experience we had in what we now call 'the brown months' was the night Angee had a stealth poo. In the middle of the night that is. Both of us deeply asleep, Ali probably dreaming of me, me probably dreaming of Michaela Strachan, when a stench, a stench the dead could not have slept through, awoke us both. A stench that simply could not be ignored and left until the morning.

The turning on of our bedside lamps in no way diminished the horror that our befuddled, sleep weary minds, had already envisioned. Poo. Poo everywhere. A poo covered nightmare. One, in which Angee had happily snuggled down and gone to sleep in.

The bed was stripped and Angee showered. We cleaned

ourselves up, had a shot of whiskey, a quick cry, another shot of whiskey, then back to bed. Who the hell thought a cat sanctuary was a clever idea? I think it was Ali, yeah let's say it was Ali's stupid idea.

As with a lot of periods in our life we may consider as 'downers' they invariably end and brighter skies soon emerge. And so it was with Angee, the infection cleared up and now only on the odd occasion is the RPR required. (Rapid Poo Response)

Perhaps I have spent overlong on the whole subject of poo but it was traumatising at the time and it's only fair that I share just a smidgeon of that trauma with you, dear reader. I do think, however, that we were particularly unlucky with the length of Angee's stomach complaint and it is in no way a reflection on all CH cats.

Ask any CH kitty owner and they will undoubtedly tell you of the sheer joy and love those kitties bring to their family. Some have even gone on to homing CH cats exclusively. You find that with the more special cats in your care, and CH kitties are undeniably that, the love between you and them becomes that bit more special too. We often feel if people could just get past what they perceive, open their hearts to a puss with a difference, they would soon see that the rewards are many and the negatives few.

*I am more than open to the suggestion of offers on Angee. In fact, I will actually pay you to take her. Don't tell Ali.

Chapter 24 – Master Alfonso Yappalot

Meet Alfie... (Alfonso, Alfafa, Yappalot)

Alfie is one of our few kids who gets a chapter all to himself. His story is more than a little remarkable, as it's an incredible battle for survival; an account of overcoming hardship and adversity and only really comparable to that of Darwin's tale of true tenacity for life. Alfie became, and remains so, one of our greatest success stories.

In the spring of 2019 and lost in a world of my own, probably daydreaming about a life with no cats and one in which I could still afford new underpants, I was busily mowing our large lawn when something in the periphery of my vision caught my attention. Among the brambles and nettles which edge the lawn, I caught the flash of something black and white. Turning off the mower and just a little curious I went to investigate. Hidden within the greenery, quite difficult to make out properly, lay a cat, and it wasn't one of ours. I could, however, see that there was something very, very, wrong with it.

Not wishing to frighten the poor thing, I ran to the house and fetched Ali, who dropped what she was doing and joined me to assess this little pussycat. By the time we got back he had gone. However, a little searching uncovered him just a little further along one of the hedgerows abutting the fields surrounding our house. In no time at all and with softly spoken words of reassurance the mystery cat was in Ali's arms and being carried back to the house where we figured we could get a proper look at him.

And what a sorry sight he was.

Again, very much like Darwin, I have never seen a cat look so damaged that it looked like it had no right to still be alive. He had obviously at some point damaged one of his rear legs. This leg was hanging oddly. It was scrawny, much scraped and battered, ending in a foot that was bloody and raw. The rest of his body wasn't in great shape either. He was severely emaciated and his fur was a mass of tangles and tats. To all intents and purposes, he looked like a puss not long for this world.

Two mysteries remain to this day. Firstly, we have no idea how this horrible injury came about. Secondly, especially considering our somewhat remote location, how he had managed to end up in our garden. Perhaps there is a divine force out there, one that helps those pure of spirit, as surely as only animals are. A force that guided this poor cat to the one place that could hopefully get him sorted out. It's a nice thought and just maybe it's true.

Handling him as carefully as possible, we hotfooted it to the vets where a thorough examination could hopefully determine the extent of the damage and if a prognosis of survival was likely. It turned out not to be very likely at all.

In addition to the obvious horrific injury to his leg, a scan turned up something neither of us had ever even heard of before. His stomach contained dirt and stones! The damage to the leg was not actually a fresh injury at all. It was, in fact, an injury that had become worse over time with a lot of necrotic tissue having formed, where he dragged it behind him. Obviously with an injury like this, his ability to hunt had been curtailed and in hunger and desperation, simply to stay alive, he had been eating earth and stones to just fill his empty belly. Our hearts broke for the plight of this poor boy and what he had been through.

The vets advised us not to get our hopes up, and with him now on pain medication and fluids to replace any lost nourishment, we left him in their more than capable hands.

Obviously, Alfie, as he was eventually called, had to have the leg removed but the one thing that really sticks in my mind from the whole episode was his complete stoicism. If you or I were in a comparable situation with a leg like that, we would surely be shouting blue murder at anyone who even dared to come close to us, let alone prodding and poking the rest of our bodies. Not so Alfie. Although part of his amenable reaction may be put down to shock, I think there was also a measure of weary resignation, knowing, on some level how grievously ill he was and that fighting any attempts at care for him was both futile and pointless.

Like I said, the origin of his injuries remains unclear but our vet put forth some theories as to how they 'may' have occurred. To start with, after having been thoroughly examined, it was discovered he only had one testicle, very odd in itself, possibly the victim of an attempted home neuter, one which had damaged the nerves on his back end and led to his present state. The injuries were simply not consistent with a car accident so another theory was put forward that someone may have kicked him. Kicked mind you, extremely hard. Hard enough to cause the damage we now had to deal with. I would not overly question either possibility as having witnessed first-hand the cruelty of some people to animals, nothing surprises me anymore.

Alfie's recuperation at the vets was neither swift or straightforward. It was beset with complications, highs, and lows. For many days, his life hung in the balance. With the damage to his leg, came the potential problems of permanent nerve damage, especially to the poor boy's plumbing. Happily, he had slowly started to regain weight but in addition to everything he had already suffered, he then had to endure the indignities of having his bladder expressed daily and his regular 'kitty colonic.' With his long-term prognosis still unclear, he was at last pronounced, hopefully out of the woods and he was able to come home for his continued care.

The picture of Alfie at the start of this chapter, gives you at least some idea of the sorry state he was in. Because he was so weak and still so very underweight, the decision to remove his leg was delayed. It was an operation that needed to be carried out when he was both fitter and fatter. Coping with his basic needs was relatively straight forward but the ever-present threat of sepsis posed a problem. The ingenious idea from our vets of using Manuka honey to smother the open wound, worked a treat. Another added notch on our never-ending learning curve, it really is simply incredible stuff.

In a matter of weeks, with Alfie's overall health started to improve and having gained some weight, his leg was removed successfully. This still led us to the thorny problem of him pooping unaided which was continuing to be an issue. Up until now this had only been remedied by yet another trip to the vets and those poor people having to give him an enema. Slowly but surely though, he started to regain some sensation and at least attempted to poop on his own. When I say in those early days there were times we had to 'help him out' with this, well I'll just leave that to your imaginations. Suffice to say, there are still nights I wake up screaming.

I would be remiss, again, at this point, if I didn't give at least an honourable mention to one of the lovely veterinary nurses, Dinny. The lovely Dinny often stepped up to undertake the unenviable task of Alfie's enema, quite frankly a smelly and disgusting job. Sadly, and inexplicably, Dinny has since relocated to Albania with the strict instructions none of the remaining staff are to give us her forwarding address. We miss her greatly but rumour has it that she found God and joined a nunnery. Apparently, the horrors of the world became too much for her and she now spends her day in prayerful contemplation. Bless her, I blame the internet.

Anyway...

What followed, was roughly three months of round the clock care and attention, as we nursed Alfie back to full health. At the beginning because he was completely immobile, we literally had to wait on him hand and foot. A permanent bed was positioned right in front of the open fire, food and water were placed readily to hand (paw), as was a litter tray, in the vain hope 'things would get moving again.' The day of his first poo is still one we remember well, an involuntary tumultuous cheer from us greeting his first turd curling out in God knows how long. From the look on his face, you would think he had won a bloody Pride of Britain award.

Because the joint venture of treatment, and care, between us and our amazing vets, actually worked, although yes, the entire process was both stressful and expensive, we would of course do it all again in a heart-beat.

With perhaps only one caveat.

Unbeknown to us, I mean how were we to know, that in the process of healing Alfie we had also created a monster. A yapping abomination that remains to this day.

Let me explain.

Alfie's rehabilitation was very lengthy, I don't wish for one minute to underplay our boy's dreadful part in this situation, the pain and especially the frustration at laying prone for so long must have been awful. But during this period, a certain amount of 'conditioning' began to occur. That is to say WE were conditioned.

Alfie soon learned that if, for example, his food bowl needed topping up, he had but simply to miaow. The same went for moving to his litter tray. And again if he wanted his ear scratched. Or he was bored. Or simply wanting to know we were still paying attention. With him being so ill, we met these ever-increasing demands with a stoicism all of our very own, albeit with a fixed grin and starting to wonder what the yappy bastard wanted next. Rinse and repeat ad infinitum.

As the months wore on, the first signs began to appear that he might well and truly be ripping the piss. Seriously, a lot of the time he was yapping for no discernible reason whatsoever, purely enjoying Mum and Dad being at his beck and call. Happily, for us at least, with strength and weight regained, he took to finding his way about on three legs; as any experienced owners out there will testify, a process that takes no time at all.

Life, once again, was restored to a semblance of normality and in what seemed no time at all, he was looking to start exploring the outside world again. Still unaware of his previous history we were extremely hesitant about this, even considered making him an indoor cat only but his spirit was determined and his god-awful yowling at the door was completely doing our heads in, so we relented.

Our fears came to nought inasmuch as he has never strayed that far from the house, seemingly happy and content with our garden and yard and the occasional nap in the fields. The lack of a leg didn't seem to bother him at all either. He was soon scooting around with the rest of them, easily navigating lower obstacles, such as gates and walls. He has even developed the delightful habit of doing a type of headstand, balanced on his front legs, and randomly spraying his scent here there and everywhere. I have witnesses this on numerous occasions now and have noticed that half the time the wee just dribbles down the back of his 'trousers.' I haven't the heart to tell him, I have to leave the lad with some vestige of pride.

The yapping however has never stopped, if anything, it's gotten worse. He yaps to be let out. He yaps to be let back in. He yaps for his breakfast, dinner, and tea. He yaps just because he enjoys yapping. I have never known such a bloody noisy cat. He completely fails to understand that he is no longer knocking on death's door and that yapping incessantly won't immediately make mum and dad come running. To you, dear reader, it may seem that this is nothing more than a sweet affectation and one to which we may be overreacting. But believe me at 5am and before you have even had a sniff of your first coffee, that noise goes through your head like a chuffing buzzsaw in an empty tin bath.

With that minor, well maybe not all that minor, consideration aside, he is a wonderfully colourful character. He is a huge part of the family and a massive snugglepuss to boot. More importantly, he is a testament to the sheer indomitable strength of a cat and what can be achieved with both excellent veterinarian care and oodles and oodles of love. I have written the prior sentence at 2.45pm with the sun out in a blue sky and all is well with the world. Had I however written it at 5.30 pm, when he has just started his antics, it would have probably been more in the vein of wondering how many pairs of black and white slipper's I could make out of him.

Our beautiful boy now, fit, and healthy albeit very noisy.

Chapter 25 – And Just Like That Your Life, As You Knew It, Is Over

***Dexter demanding proof, any proof whatsoever,
that he had been in the butter***

Okay I'll concede that one, maybe two, even three, cats may not noticeably impact your life and you may be able to maintain your everyday existence virtually unimpeded. Any more than that though, and you are basically screwed.

I like a comparison that has often been circulated; that keeping cats is like joining the mafia, easier to get in to than it is to leave. Of course, you may never awake to a horse's severed head on the pillow beside you but a mouse spleen in your shoes surely amounts to the same thing.

Never again will you be able to leave the house without worrying about a stray cat hair on your best clothes. There will absolutely be hair on your bloody clothes. That stuff gets freaking everywhere. Now though, it becomes an exercise in damage limitation, one that you will seldom, if ever, win. You will, in all likelihood, cancel your plans, stick on your comfies, and watch TV with Tiddles on your lap wearing a knowing smile.

And on the occasions when you do manage to make it out of the house, your return will inevitably include the question, 'Can you smell piss?' This proceeds in one of two ways. You either do smell piss and spend the next half hour finding the errant urine and cleaning it. Or you don't and then question whether you have actually lost your sense of smell completely and spend the next half hour looking for an errant puddle that may or may not exist. Schrodinger's piss, if you will. Either way, Tiddles will be somewhere nearby, laughing at your efforts and thinking about what a pathetic species humankind is and how the power of the feline is omnipotent.

Holidays will become tricky affairs also, as you only have two choices. Firstly, you can book all of your kitties into a cattery, hope they don't blacken the family name and on your return be prepared for them to express their indignation and anger at being abandoned in such a manner. This may go on for some time. And believe, me a scorned woman doesn't hold a candle to a pissed off cat that thinks it's been wronged. Secondly, you can hire a cat sitter to stay at your house and provide for all their needs in your absence. This second approach may or may not work. It could be the case your gang are happy with the sitter and your departure and return are seamlessly achieved. Alternatively, they may hate the sitter and embark on a series of dirty protests. Worse still, the sitter may be a nosey little bugger and find your collection of dildos and post a picture of them online entitled 'Who lives in a house like this?' It could happen.

Eating in peace is another simple pleasure that you will sacrifice. You may have prepared and cooked a relative smorgasbord of choice cuts and only the very tenderest of meats for your delinquent horde to tuck into. But you will certainly still find those pathetic, sorrowful eyes looking up at you, clearly starved, as you prepare to take the last mouthful of your beans on toast. Those simpering eyes will not be denied. In fact, the wee bastard has probably just gone and taken a massive dump to make room for the last morsel of your dinner.

A peaceful night's sleep, oh grasshopper, you silly little thing, for those nights have fled forever. It wouldn't be so bad if Tiddles just settled down in one spot, curled up and slept for a solid eight hours. Not a chance. Your bed will become the equivalent of musical chairs. A game that is, where you're not invited to play and where your very existence is ignored. Throughout the night, you will be clambered over, sat on, and quite possibly become an involuntary participant in a fun game of WWE wrestling.

But it doesn't end there.

Even when you do manage to fall asleep, you will almost certainly be woken at some ungodly hour by a pilchard-breathed moggy shouting in your face, demanding you get up and make his breakfast. Which, depending on his mood, he may or may not even bloody well eat. On the rare occasion you 'out sleep' Tiddles, the waking experience is not, by any means, guaranteed to be a pleasant one. With no concept whatsoever of personal space, Tiddles may have decided that, in order to waken you, they should first get in your face. I have lost count of the times my bleary eyes have opened to the sight (up close and personal) of a hairy bum and little else. That sentence does rather neatly lend itself to a gag about my wife but sadly, I'm just not that brave.

Cats too, unfortunately, do not always make for the best of relationships with neighbours. It may be that your cats have taken to having their after-dinner poo in the bed of his prize roses or that they have decimated the local birdlife that he has, for so many years, lovingly fed and provided nesting boxes for.

In either situation, let's face it, Tiddles is banged to rights and guilty of all the above. Again, you are left with just two choices. Firstly, you can lie. You can profess your puzzlement as to where all these cats are coming from and wholeheartedly agree they are indeed pests and noncommittedly comment about how 'this sort of thing shouldn't be allowed.' However, lies can quickly unravel and your neighbour might not necessarily be a genius but can put 2 and 2 together when he sees Tiddles waving at him from your bedroom window. The alternative is just to move. The latter is preferable if you ask me. Who wants to live next to someone who doesn't like cats? Your neighbour is an idiot, probably wears sandals with socks too.

Single? I wish you God speed. Any potential suitor will first have to get past Tiddles and gang. An unenviable ask, because, in order to gain their approval, they will have to either be made of solid cheese or willing to approach your cats with a deferential disposition in body and thought. Cats particularly liked being either bowed or curtsied to. If for some implausible reason your possible new mate decides to get amorous, then I suggest you go back and re-read the chapter entitled 'No sex please we have cats.' Tiddles and co will almost certainly ruin any magical moment and probably throw up just in time to coincide with your 'big finish.'

Disposable income vanishes as any 'spare' income invariably gets spent on them. You may wish to invest in a set of ladders, as at some point Tiddles WILL get stuck up a tree or on the roof. Cleaning products will become your new best friends and the vet will be programmed into your phone on speed dial. There will be paw prints in the butter and furballs on your fresh clean duvet. Seriously, the list goes on and on. I do hope that I'm not putting any of you off the idea of 'enjoying' a multi-cat household, it's merely that I wish you all to be fully aware. Well, as aware as possible that is, of the many eventualities you may face. The above list is by no means exhaustive.

Indeed, to travel down this road is to see it as a one-way street; one in which the street lights slowly blink off, one after another, behind you. Perhaps in your innocence and naivety though, you think I overegg or perhaps exaggerate the situation? Please be assured that some of your fellow readers will already have embarked on this journey of no return. Picture them reading along as they sagely nod in agreement. They may be taking a 'nip' from their ever-handy hip flask as they wonder when, exactly, did that nervous twitch in the eye start? To them I say: I hear you my sisters, I'm with you my brothers and all in between. I would welcome you in a warm embrace of empathy if I could. Well, actually even if I could I probably wouldn't. Ya know, what with not really liking people and all.

Chapter 26 – On Dealing With Sorrow And The Rainbow Bridge

Just some of the kids' caskets. As you can see for yourself, heart-breaking as it is, there's not a lot of room left on top of the kitchen cupboards.

I can deal with piss. I can deal with poo. I can deal with puke. I can even deal with random critter innards stuck to the bottom of my shoe. I cannot, however, deal with an animal dying. And that applies if said animal is feline or otherwise.

I am completely useless at it. I don't know what to say or how to behave. My whole 'pragmatic' approach flies out of the window and I am left floundering in helplessness. My normal go-to status of cracking a gag is both inadequate and wholly inappropriate.

Part of the answer, I think, undoubtedly lies in a man's self-designated role as 'fixer.' This role is both a strength and a point for improvement, depending on the situation. However, in this instance, it simply doesn't apply. There are just some things in life that cannot be fixed.

Whether it be that one of our kids has met with an accident or we have to accompany them on their final journey; experience to date has shown I have to confront the finality and immediate effects of death on two fronts. The first one being Ali.

Now my wife is hard as nails. She has a no-nonsense approach to both life and people but when it comes to the animals, she can fall apart at the drop of a hat. She will always approach their care with determination and patience but once the scales have tipped and the end of their journey is in sight, then the floodgates open. At such times I am a little envious of her ability to display her feelings so openly.

In the situation of a cat that needs some help to the other side via euthanasia, Ali will invariably be there, stroking the baba with tears streaming down her face, only giving vent to full sobs when the cat's life has departed. Meanwhile, I am standing there with the stupid British stiff upper lip. The painful lump in my throat feeling like the size of a tennis ball, all the while trying to hold back tears that absolutely no one there would give a single toss I shed. If this behaviour is how society has decreed a man should behave, then it's bloody pathetic.

To date there has only been one exception to this.

***

In the early days of TC's, a beautiful black girl came to live with and her name was Hugs. I'm not sure exactly why or how but the two of us bonded closely and she soon became a favourite of mine. She developed cancer, an inoperable cancer that went on to shorten the life of my gorgeous girl. Had she not developed this horrid condition, she would most assuredly still be with us, curled up on her favourite window sill and still calling out with her distinctive miaow for luffs and treats. I'm starting to feel teary just writing about her.

Despite giving her the best care available, it reached the stage where she no longer had any inclination to eat or drink. She was losing weight rapidly and was in pain, so it would have been a cruelty and not a kindness to try and extend her life further. On her last journey to the vets, it was agreed that this was one baby who would be in MY arms as she departed this world.

As the vet administered first the sedative, followed by the lethal injection, I softly spoke words of love to her, stroking her beautifully soft, black fur. I'm by no means a noisy crier but I do remember the tears streaming down my face, completely unstoppable. For once I didn't actually care. Being present when a life, any life, passes, is an experience like no other.

But back to Ali...

My first instinct is always to comfort her and while I do, I am happy to put my own grief on the back-burner. Obviously, there is nothing I can do to bring the dead loved one back to life but I can at least seek to reassure her. This usually involves talking about what a wonderful life our latest passed kitty got to enjoy. I remind her what an awesome mummy she was to them and I provide whatever hugs and cuddles are required. The words may change a little each time but the platitudes are essentially the same. You would have to ask Ali whether my attempts at reassurance help at all but to me they always seem woefully inadequate.

After this, if at all, I will turn attention to my grief and try to deconstruct it.

Now, not all of the deaths are the same though. Sometimes I find it easier to take a philosophical approach. This is often the case if you are dealing with an older cat and one who possibly has had numerous underlying health conditions. Very much as when an older person dies, you can celebrate a life lived. There may even be a bit of anticipation of the inevitable that your mind has already prepared you for. Not so with a younger animal, who should have plenty of life ahead and who you may feel has been 'snatched' away too soon. Primarily, these are the occasions that I really struggle with.

At these times, I know that my reaction is wholly unhealthy. Particularly in the case of a young cat, or one I feel I have a special bond with. I pop the event of their death in a box in my head and simply refuse to remove the lid and have a peek. Almost as if the cat had never existed. Memories only coming unbidden when perhaps a conversation mentions them or an old photo comes to light. This is clearly not the ideal method of dealing with death and grief but it's now a coping mechanism that has become my default. Having dealt with so much death, our worst run being four babies in eleven weeks, it's not a reaction I can see myself changing anytime soon. I think the alternative would be sitting in a darkened room for days on end sucking my thumb and dwelling on the unfairness of life, wondering why bad things happen to good people.

Inevitably, this subject can lead us to a conversation about spirituality. Having had religion thrust down my throat from an early age, this is a subject towards which I now have more than a little antipathy. Perhaps bundling up religion and spirituality together is a little unfair but my life's experience has taught me there is often little to separate the two. That was, until I learned of The Rainbow Bridge.

Now, when someone close to us dies, whatever kind of soul it may be, we reach for solace wherever we can find it. We look for it in places that in normal times, we would dismiss as mere frippery. The idea, notion, of The Rainbow Bridge came to my attention in the early days of our rescue. This is a belief held dear by animal lovers the world over. For those still unaware of this belief, or maybe just the exact details, I will try my best to describe it.

The original idea of this mystical bridge came in the form of a couple of poems written in the 1980's and 1990's but with their roots in Norse mythology. They describe a beautiful meadow where all dead animals go; a place where there is no pain or suffering and everyone is well fed and happy. The only unrequited yearning of these animals is the sense of loss they feel for their owners. These owners will join them upon their own deaths. After enjoying a wondrous reunion, the animals and their human companions cross The Rainbow Bridge together, into whatever eternal blissful type heaven awaits at the other end.

Sounds far-fetched right? Sounds like a fantasy for the feeble-minded, vulnerable and those in need of some succour regardless of how fantastical it may be. A fictitious construct to allay hurt feelings and nothing more. The clinical, cold part of me from yesteryear may well have concurred with that assessment, but not anymore.

To start with, animals are as near as you can get to what would be considered a 'pure soul.' There is simply no such thing as a bad animal. Any perceived 'bad deed' perpetrated by an animal can either be attributed to its innate behaviour or because of some sort of human intervention. Animals react and when they react in a way which we would consider bad, then there has almost always been a person in that animal's life who has bought the worst out in it. A person who, for the most part, isn't fit to be anywhere near an animal in the first place. Ask a rescuer, any rescuer and each will confirm that the majority of behavioural issues we have to deal are as the result of human interference. People should have to pass some sort of test before being allowed an animal of their own. Some of the things we have witnessed make you wonder how they conduct satisfying and healthy relationships with other people. They probably don't.

So yes, a pure soul, not at all absurd when you think about beliefs put forward for when a human dies. All kinds of notions by all kinds of faiths concern, often in some detail, what may or may not happen in the supposed afterlife. Some of these even surpass the details of The Rainbow Bridge's paradisaic conditions, be it endless virgins for your delectation or forever singing the praises of God whilst simultaneously polishing the stars. Conversely, most of these nirvana-like states have some dark counterpoint, a direct opposite enjoyed by the faithful's heavenly rewards. For instance, have you ever been to a funeral where the minister has even hinted at the recently deceased being on a one-way trip to hell, despite you knowing they were a complete bastard when they were alive? No, me neither.

Delusion can be a many splendored thing.

Also for consideration is the science. Something I will give you a dumbed down version of because, quite honestly, the dumbed down version is the only one I understand.

All life is made up of energy and physics has proven that energy cannot be destroyed. Here, for me, the ground becomes a little shaky. Energy can neither be created nor destroyed, at best it can be stored. Life force is certainly an energy, so when something/someone dies, where does the energy go? Don't look at me, I was on quicksand about three sentences ago, so that grainy goop has just closed over the top of my head and Tarzan isn't in sight to throw me a vine and drag me out.

Perhaps though, just perhaps, that energy is now vibrating on a different level, maybe in a different place, maybe in the peace and tranquillity of the meadow at The Rainbow Bridge. Don't dismiss the idea out of hand, because of course that same energy could well be your uncle George feasting with the Vikings in Valhalla or your aunt Edna, right now trimming Satan's toenails.

So yes, sorrow is a painful subject and an even more painful ordeal to go through. One which each of us deals with differently, because the pain for each of us is different. There are no rules to it. Whatever gets you by, whatever helps minimise that godawful heartache and move on with your life. And The

Rainbow Bridge, well why not? If anyone deserves a beautiful afterlife, something more than this life on earth, then surely, it's those perfect animal souls that we are privileged to share our lives with.

Normally, wishing to end a chapter on a positive or light-hearted note, I would finish there but instead I would like to conclude by asking a favour. And it is this.

If at some point you have to take your furry on that final journey to the vet, then please, PLEASE make sure you are with them all the way.

Some people have said that they couldn't possibly go through that experience but please be assured that your feelings pale in comparison to that of your pets.

YOU are your furry's world. You are its everything. They deserve more at the end of their life than to depart from this world in a strange room with a relatively strange person. It is even proven that, by your very presence alone, you can lower your baba's heartrate, one which will surely be beating like a paradiddle.

However hard this situation may be please rise to the occasion. This is, after all, the very last act of love that you can show them.

Chapter 27 – My Heart Is No Longer Mine (Part II)

*Meet Blossom (Bloss, Somey, Cock-Block)

Blossom is perhaps the most beautiful tabby ever to grace this world. And I mean past, present or future. Her words, not mine but a sentiment I agree with wholeheartedly. Oh yeah, she also has the cutest button nose you could ever wish to see.

This fascinating femme of fluff was the second official TC's cat, coming to us after her owner moved abroad. Unbelievable as it sounds, she didn't come from a world-renowned breeder, specialising in dazzling perfection. I mean, look at her!!! Blossom was actually part of a farmyard litter of kittens. Supposedly half wild, we were assured that despite her having a wee body that looked made for cuddles and snuggles, she would never be a lap cat. Her first couple of eventful weeks with us certainly gave this description a ring of truth to it. I should amend that to her first couple of weeks WITHOUT us.

Very early in her probationary period, during her indoor orientation as it were, she somehow managed to escape. Escape that is, to a bloody great big gorse bush in a field beside the house. We only became aware of this when frantically searching for her. As the daylight was starting to fade, a pitiful miaowing came blowing to us in the wind. Having triangulated the source of the sound, we spent the next several hours on hands and knees, torches clenched between our teeth, equally calling her name accompanied with terms of endearment and roundly cursing all cats ever born. With grit and determination, we eventually managed to catch her. To this day, we still bear the scratch and bite marks to hands, arms, and faces. A couple of days later, she escaped again.

I should interject at this point that trying to catch any cat that doesn't want to be caught is, at best, an exercise in patience and at worst one in futility. The task at hand is made considerably more difficult when the cat doesn't really know you. This makes apprehension nigh on impossible. But God loves a trier and bloody hell did we try.

The following week or two became a comedy of errors, a French farce, where the ever-elusive Blossom led us up the garden path, back down it again, and more than once into the middle of a bloody gorse patch or two. Having put up some missing posters and with the forbearance of some very patient neighbours, we managed to track down her movements and some potential hidey-holes she might be sleeping in. It was time to up the ante and introduce the cat trap.

This, dear reader, backfired spectacularly.

For those of you unfamiliar with the basic cat trap, I will describe it. It's a long contraption made of metal wire mesh with a spring sensitive trap lever at one end which, when depressed, sets off a mechanism, dropping a door behind the nosey, and now entrapped, cat. For the trap to work effectively, you lace the trap lever with the smelliest and most enticing titbits available. Tuna or pilchards score superbly well on all points.

The trap worked a dream.... on every neighbour's cat within a two-mile radius and on several occasions one of ours. Not once, mind you, did it work on Blossom.

Although we saw Blossom several times over the following twelve days, once I even managed to grab a scruff of her tail, the damned furry scarlet pimpernel continued to prove elusive. We began to give up hope of ever catching her. We even travelled the 5 miles to her previous home on several occasions but no sight or sound had been glimpsed by her previous neighbours. You really do start running out of ideas.

Having become a little dejected at the idea of never having her come home again and with a house full of furries still to look after, life carried on. That is, until one night I went to put the chickens to bed and spied the wee minx in their garden. A little stunned but with a sense of renewed hope, I stealthily crept back to the house to ask Ali how we should proceed. Not wanting to 'scare her off,' it was decided Ali would approach her alone, armed with a bag of Dreamies and pocket-full of good intentions.

I was more than a little flabbergasted when, a short time later, Ali appeared with Blossom contentedly snuggled in her arms. She had shown no signs of the former ball of fury and had happily been picked up and carried into the house. Whereupon, she dutifully tucked in to a fresh bowl of food. She never tried to run away again.

If that doesn't explain to you the sheer bloody-mindedness and contrary nature of bastard cats, I have no words left that will.

With her early shenanigans soon forgotten, we got to knowing Blossom properly. To our delight, not only was she a lap cat but a lap cat supreme. In fact, I would say, that her love for her 'luffs' now only comes second to how much she loves herself. I don't wish to cast any aspersions on her previous owner, perhaps suggesting I am somehow a better person or have a 'softer touch' but I will say I am a better person and almost certainly have a softer touch.

Cats. Basically, you get what you give.

Over time we both fell head over heels in love with Blossom. Even her thinly veiled snobbery is a mere affectation and just adds to her charm. She simply refuses to eat with the riffraff and will patiently wait by a door, with a cat flap in it, until you open the door. She knows how to use cat flaps, I've seen her. She just flatly refuses to use them unless she absolutely has to (no handy hooman to open the door) deeming them to be just one of many things that are 'beneath' her.

Whilst Ali and Blossom have a wonderful relationship all of their own, mine and Blossom's developed in to something special, as a result of Ali's 'spreading the love.' A judicious process which involves her giving each of our kids an equal amount of time and attention. For an attention hungry sap like myself, who considers the day a cat even looks at me to be a life-affirming event, Blossom singling me out as her paramour was like all my Christmases coming at once. I'm pathetically needy when it comes to the cats' attention and Blossom pounced on that weakness and has exploited it fully for the last 7 years.

The photo of her majesty at the start of this chapter is a common sight of an evening when we finish for the day. We wind down for a couple of hours in front of the TV, before going to bed. Custom dictates that Blossom paws my mouth, with just enough extended claw to hurt and this is my cue to start petting her. Should I stop for any reason, maybe choking on a Crunchie for example (this did happen one time), I get a gentle bop as a reminder to continue my ministrations whilst she gives me a firm look of disapproval that luff time is a contiguous affair and should only be paused under the direst of circumstances. Obviously, my death by delicious Cadburys chocolate notwithstanding.

So perfect is she who must be obeyed, that even tats, a curse for all slaves of long-haired cats, don't properly attach. With just a little gentle teasing they slide free, something that she happily deigns to let you do. Her beauty is blatantly more important than any momentary discomfort. If I had to, for the sake of balance, mention one minor blemish in her overall loveliness, it would be that poop does sometimes stick to the fur on her bum. Surely though, this a problem that affects the great and good? What is the odd dangle-berry between friends? Still, I'm not comfortable at her finding out I have broadcast this but am reasonably sure she can't read, so I think I'm safe.

The day is invariably rounded off with me reading in bed and Blossom gently purring in my ear, readying herself for when I'm done. Having removed my glasses and put my book away, she then assumes position atop my head whereupon I fall asleep to the thunderous cacophony of her snores vibrating through my skull.

So yes, in the inner-most part of this cynical and pragmatic cat man, beats a heart which has been captured not once but twice. I cannot countenance the death of either of my girls, yet I would be blind not to see that age has begun to leave its mark on each of them. My hope is that I go first, thereby saving myself the pain of their parting; a parting that there will no box big enough to contain. Maybe they could even eulogise about how much they loved me; how their daddy was always there with luffs and attention when needed. Maybe they could lament that, although I was a mug for a pretty face and sassy attitude, I was still their mug.

Chapter 28 – But Seriously

This picture was taken on the last day Tc was with us. Holding a cat this way is known as 'babying' and is the true test of trust (mostly theirs) between a puss and its hooman. This hold should not be approached without a degree of caution. I had NEVER babied Tc before. Whether he was simply too weak to fight off my unwanted attentions or, knowing he only had a fleeting time left in this world and passively 'gave in,' I will never know. I'm glad we had that moment.

Entitling a chapter 'But seriously,' from a bloke who has spent the last 20 odd chapters basically ripping the piss, may seem like a juxtaposition. But when it comes to certain aspects of cat care, any animal care for that matter, a few subjects need a degree of brevity.

Neutering.

There is a myth that has circulated for many years around it being 'good for a cat' to have at least one litter of kittens. I have no idea how this notion first gained traction but it is absolute claptrap. Rescues and sanctuaries throughout the world are full to brimming with unwanted, many abused, kittens and cats. The world does not need any more. Knowingly allowing your cat to get pregnant is irresponsible and you could well start a chain reaction that leads to hundreds more kittens. A problem you won't have to personally deal with but believe me, someone else will. Don't get me wrong, there is nothing cuter than a fresh batch of doe-eyed little balls of fluff but if this is what you are basing your reasoning on, you would be just as well buying a litter of stuffed toys. Far cheaper and they won't destroy your curtains or wooden floors.

The subject of neutering encompasses far more than that of just unwanted propagation. There are many health benefits too. It adds to the lowering of aggression and can help alleviate many, often 'messy,' behavioural issues. So be it boy or girl, don't delay and get that cat neutered ASAP!

A subject that is dear to our hearts is the feral cat.

You would be very surprised indeed, as was I, to know of the relative army out there whose sole-focus is the giving of care and love to the many feral colonies that exist. These unsung heroes spend an inordinate amount of time trapping, neutering, and feeding these cats. Cats, that is, who would never be suitable as house cats or comfortable being domesticated. These people often work in the wee hours and fund this care out of their own pockets. Simply put, they are driven purely by their love for animals. They are seldom recognised by the community and even less so by the cats in their care. A feral cat's life is an extremely hard one but because of the ministrations of these carers, at the very sharp end of rescue, their lives can be extended. In many cases, they will have a reasonable life expectancy that they otherwise would not.

You may well be thinking that this is all very nice but

what does that have to do with me? Well in all likelihood, unbeknownst to you, there could very well be one of these selfless volunteers operating in your area. Established rescues are often the first port of call in receiving aid and support from the public. However, the people who look after feral colonies are overlooked. As TC's is self-funded, I can assure you, from experience, that they too, would welcome donations. These could contribute to petrol money or general overheads. Maybe you have some old towels? Those are always useful, or perhaps you'd like to volunteer your physical help. All of these things would be gratefully received. In addition to their work with feral cats, many of these people also juggle the responsibilities of a hectic home life. Dropping them a message of appreciation and support when you think of it, I promise, will be received warmly. After all, apart from a little time on your behalf, that costs nothing at all.

Another subject worthy of mention is that of volunteering.

We ourselves have been blessed with a beautiful young lady called Becca, who visits with us twice a week and who has got herself involved in all aspects of looking after the kids. She has proved herself to be utterly invaluable because an extra pair of hands regularly helping, is vital to the smooth running of a rescue. And that is the crux of the matter with many rescues. We are constantly busy, and it can regularly seem like there are not enough hours in the day to get everything done.

Now you may have a horror scenario in your head of giving up some of your precious free time, only to find yourself in a cold, dirty pen, on your hands and knees, cleaning out litter trays. Obviously rescue has that side to things and I would be lying to say otherwise. But equally important, perhaps even more importantly, is the socialisation of the animals in this aforementioned 'high stress' environment. Simply spending time with cats in a rescue is a job all by itself. It can help lower their anxiety (not to mention yours), help with any behavioural issues and hopefully make those cats more likely to find a forever home. Time spent with a cat really is never wasted.

If you find yourself with a little spare time and inclination, then why not reach out to a rescue near you? Find out what they require and whether you feel you are suitable candidate to fulfil those needs. You will almost certainly find a niche that is perfect for you and there are few roles which you will find as rewarding. Again, it costs you nothing to ask and may well open up a new world to you, full of like-minded people and gratifying labour.

Next, your cats MOT.

At the very least, your beloved puss needs an annual once-over. They need to be inoculated against many of the nasty viruses that circulate through the feline species and they need a general health assessment. This will give you peace of mind that Tiddles is happy and healthy. Playing the waiting game until something is visibly wrong, is both lazy and short-sighted, not to mention a false economy. Any health problem caught early is often easier to treat than one left to fester and grow. This could be something as simple as a couple of teeth that need descaling for the minimal cost of a dental check. This easy job will almost certainly save Tiddles (and your wallet) from unnecessary pain. It could be the relatively easy removal of a small growth before it becomes the heartache and anguish of an inoperable tumour, indicating the end for Tiddles. Vets aren't infallible but they are your first line of defence in professional care and would much rather see you and your companion animal(s) frequently, in fine fettle than rarely and with them having to give you unwelcome news.

Meeting your cat's needs.

Years ago, I was invited to a friend's house for dinner. During the obligatory pre-meal chitchat, I was more than a little distracted by the smells of a freshly cooking chicken coming from the kitchen. It truly was a mouth-watering scent and

I eagerly awaited the approaching meal. Disappointment is a word that doesn't come close to describing how I felt when I was presented with a distinctly average Spag Bol and the resident Tiddles tucked in to the delicious roasted bird.

Some of you may shrug at this story, it being a regular occurrence in your house. Your own personal Tiddles may rule the roost and receive only the absolute supreme delicacies for their dinner. Well, fair play to you but not everyone holds their own Tiddles in such high esteem.

Cats do like the finer things in life and, even as you provide for their basic needs of food, shelter and warmth, there is no harm every now and then 'going the extra mile' to ensure their comfort and happiness.

I think the days of kicking the cat out at night are over. If not, they ought to be. It's one thing if your cat chooses to go out but forcibly ejecting it is unkind and cruel. Put yourself in their furry boots. I think you'll agree that a bed near a warm radiator on a cold winter's night is hard to beat. I feel this paragraph itself should be seen as a given but have included it purely as a reminder.

The issue of food is something that you may wish to anthropomorphise about. Bargain cat food is probably a bargain because it sucks. Nobody is asking you to cook Tiddles Michelin star rated meals every day but since variety is the spice of life, at least make their diet interesting. Established brands come in a variety of flavours/textures and, come the end of the trading day, most supermarkets will have either fresh or cooked meats heavily discounted. Obviously, live within your means, but be sure to treat your beloved Tiddles every now and then. A grateful cat is a happy cat. Allegedly.

A bored cat can be a destructive cat.

Some cats are laid-back and happy to entertain themselves; almost akin to living with a chilled out, albeit furry, roommate. Other cats, however, are attention-seeking divas who, unless attended to, will wantonly destroy, and desecrate everything you hold dear. Of course, these Tiddles types will simultaneously be endearingly wonderful. So how does one deal with THESE nut jobs?

A great bonding experience, and one that occupies your cat's time and attention, is the simple brush/comb/zoom groom. Very few cats can resist a good grooming session and nine times out ten, you will tire of it before they do. You get to connect on quite a deep level with your cat when brushing it. This can only enhance your personal relationship with Tiddles and helps keep unwanted hair around the rest of the house to a minimum. You will obviously still have hair all over that special dress or best suit you have been saving for a special occasion but if you can't accept that you should have gotten a gold fish instead.

Toys too, are a great aid in engaging with your cat and exhausting their pent-up energy. Remember though, it is only a toy when you help them play with it. Otherwise, it is a useless inanimate object. In some ways, cats have an extremely high boredom threshold and can be entertained, at times for literally hours with the simplest of things. We found these little cat friendly plastic springs that the cats lose their shit over. Those things ping here there and everywhere. Every day, they 'rediscover' them and the fun starts all over again. Don't overthink your cat's intelligence or ability to be entertained by the smallest of things, after all none of them have yet caught the red dot.

Getting a cat.

I hope I'm reading the 'room' correctly when I presume that, having gotten this far in the book, you already meet a certain demographic. Giving a cat/kitten as a present is a definite no no. If, for some reason, you have considered this and some kind of faulty reasoning on your behalf thinks it's a clever idea, then please take a long, hard look in the mirror and give yourself a good slap. It's a terrible idea and one usually undertaken by the short-sighted and feeble of mind.

Being answerable, yes that's right, answerable, for another life is not only a privilege but it's an almost sacred responsibility. That goes for any animal but as my experience is with cats, it is them I'm focusing on.

If you choose to home a kitten you are possibly looking at a 20-year project that could well cost you several thousands of pounds. If that one sentence alone scares you, (no gags at all here from me) then simply don't get one, a cat is not for you. Nor is a dog, for that matter.

If, however, you are set on getting a cat and prepared for everything it entails in providing for it, please do consider something other than a kitten. Kittens are relatively easy to home from rescues, whereas older cats often get overlooked. And unfairly so. An older cat, one with a few more miles on its clock, often comes with at least a bit of history. That history could be behavioural, medical or temperament. To a certain extent, a kitten is an unknown quantity. An older cat will be pretty set in their ways and say, for example, it's a lap cat you are looking for, well you could go to a rescue today and probably find the perfect companion straight away. Also, don't bypass the cats that are not considered 'conventionally pretty.' In an effort to have a flawless feline, one who is perfectly proportioned with beautiful symmetrical markings, many hidden gems are completely passed over. In our own personal experience, some very unremarkable looking cats, have turned out to have just the sweetest temperament and been a source of ongoing joy. Beauty is in the eye of the beholder and sometimes you just need to look past the exterior to what lays beneath and see the beauty within.

I understand too that many people can be put off by an existing medical condition in a cat, again something that might not be as dire as you first think. Heart conditions, for example, are quite common and are often remedied with just one simple pill per day. FIV too (the feline equivalent of HIV) has received a bad rap when, in reality, cats with this condition can live long happy lives in the company of other cats. Very much like their human counterparts, these cats suffer with poor immune systems and are susceptible to infections. Even when this does happen, 'fixes' are often straightforward and inexpensive. Many people will not even entertain rehoming a 'sick' cat and so these poor pusses are left languishing in rescues, sometimes for many years. Talk to the rescuer. Be prepared to 'go that extra mile' and give these cats the chance in life they undoubtedly deserve.

Cat care, whether you already have one, or are thinking of getting one, is a complex subject especially when you take into consideration the many, many variables. It's a complex subject but no more than any other long-term project you might undertake. Now years into our journey of rescue, we still straddle a never-ending learning curve and are always happy to confront any new situations and benefit from new knowledge gained. It's a never-ending process but one that hopefully you can meet with optimism rather than anxiety.

In the normal course of things, your resident puss will eat, sleep, and generally cause havoc. You may be lucky enough to have a cat that never needs any serious medical intervention or display any worrying behavioural issues. These cats do exist but in my experience are exceedingly rare. The important thing though, is to rise to the challenge when difficulties occur. A cat is not a commodity, a thing that can be dispensed of when the going gets tough, worse still, 'passed on' to become someone else's problem.

We live in a throwaway society and sadly, that has come to include animals. Whilst I feel this whole book is a 'nuts and bolts' account of the inner workings of caring for a lot of cats, many histories have been left out because of their truly horrendous nature. Invariably, each horror story involves a human.

Including this chapter has been hard for me, as my nature is light-hearted and I try and see the humour in any given situation. I could not, however, compose a cat-compendium type book without mentioning all of the above. Cats are an addition to our lives; an addition of love, fun and companionship. Understanding that with such a wonderful addition, comes a measure of responsibility and obligation. You have an obligation to care for Tiddles through both the highs and lows of life.

Each of our kids who pass to The Rainbow Bridge get their name on a stone in our memorial garden. Even though they're never far from our thoughts anyway, it's nice to have a visual prompt to remember them and their funny antics.

Every single baba that has come through the doors of TC's Forever Home has left an indelible imprint on our hearts. Some of them gave us the pleasure of their company for many years. Some were with us for hardly any time at all. Some were a delight in nearly every way and some stubborn, difficult, and contrary. Each with as different a personality as mine is to yours and each with a story of their own. This chapter is dedicated to them.

Bongo...

This is Bongo and he was our little ginger Prince. He came to live with us as a young kitten, having had a deformed leg removed after he was born. He soon became inseparable from Artemis; the two of them seemed to be glued together. Since he adapted very quickly to his missing leg, we took the decision to let him outside and it turned out to be an environment that he loved and seemed to thrive in. No matter where he had been on any given day, or what he was doing, without fail he would clamber on our bed every single night to say 'nanite' to mum and dad. Until one night, he didn't. Bongo was such a creature of habit that alarm bells instantly began to ring. We repeatedly called his name until it was completely dark and we went back to bed. We just hoped that he may have got locked in somewhere. The next day, Ali found his body in one of the fields around the house. He was so young and so perfect that devastation doesn't come close to how we felt about his death. Taking his body to the vets they found a ridiculously small cut on him; one which they deduced had led to Peritonitis. Bongo is firmly in one of my mental boxes.

Scrummy...

Madame Scrumptious Twinkletoes (Scrummy for short) joined the crew when her former owner died. She was a more 'mature' lady and already very much set in her ways. She had little patience for the other cats' nonsense and was the not least bit interested in their company. After a 'frosty' beginning, she soon thawed towards her mum and dad and happily accepted lengthy grooming sessions. These were met with a throaty purr. She sounded more like a motorbike than a cat. Our big, beautiful long-haired tortie made the bed in the spare room 'her' bed and became one of the bigger personalities in the house. She was a truly big girl when she arrived but a couple of years later, cancer got a terrible hold of her and as she started wasting away to nothing. So, we had to make the final trip with her. Another massive loss and we can't help but comment on one of her favourite sunbathing spots in one of the fields whenever we pass it.

Star...

Star was one of Ali's original brood. She was a gorgeous, petite little girl with a heart condition. As you can see from the picture, she thrived on human contact and would often do the above 'superman' to get the full benefit of a belly rub. Timid and shy by nature, she did form bonds with some of the other cats but her 'flighty' nature made her a bit of a target for the bullies in the house. Having come from Ali's terraced house, where she had been an indoor cat, when she discovered the outside world, she was delirious. She thoroughly enjoyed being outside and would travel far and wide. She was another puss who simply didn't come home one day. We have theorised that her heart eventually gave out, she had a grade 5 heart murmur, although we never found her body. Our fervent hope is that she was either asleep or having fun at the time and didn't feel a thing.

Mortimer...

This is the only picture of Mortimer that we ever got. He was a poorly, elderly puss that never even got to spend a single night with us and what a tragic story he had. We first became aware of him when a concerned resident found him in with her horses, seemingly lost and disorientated. She managed to trap him and as the local 'go to' rescue, we were contacted. In the kindest way possible, I have never seen such a pathetic looking cat. Emaciated and clearly blind, he was immediately rushed to the vets. His story just gets worse. After a thorough examination and blood tests, he was diagnosed as late stage FELV. He did not go The Rainbow Bridge alone though, because we held him tight and told him how brave he was and that he was loved. Sitting here writing this, I am crying angry tears. This poor boy, given his age and condition had, without one shadow of a doubt, been 'dumped.' Some selfish bastard figured he was too much to 'fix,' took him into the countryside and dropped him off to 'fend for himself.' An elderly, sick and blind cat left to fend for himself. I hope there is an afterlife and by extension, hell, where those responsible will suffer for the pain and anxiety meted out to this beautiful soul. Whereas most of our babies are cremated, we went against tradition with Mortimer and buried him in the garden. Now, whenever I am working near or pass his final resting place, we have a wee chat.

Queenie...

Queenie was a beautiful 18-year-old puss, who spent her remaining time on this earth with us when her former hooman mummy died. She only lived three more months after she moved in with us but quickly and happily stationed herself on the sofa (beside my spot) which she rarely left. Ever clever, as surely cats are, she had chosen the optimum spot for love and strokes when required and the choicest of morsels from dad's dinner plate. Sadly, kidney disease took her as it does with so many. We like to think she has been reunited with her true mum who she had obviously adored. I think Ali and I were only ever surrogate parents to her but that was fine, she lived the remainder of her life loved and in comfort.

Oscar...

Above is how you would probably expect a cat with end stage FIV to look. Although, he was nowhere near as poorly as he looks at the time of this photo. Our brave Oscar lived a long and full life, even if he did gain the unfortunate, although affectionately intended, moniker, of 'Zombie Cat.' Our Oscar was a complicated boy, with often contradictory personality traits. He loved love but at the same time was very particular about who touched him. He did, however, bond very firmly with several of the other cats, particularly Tc and Benny, although he mellowed in later years and was quite content to snuggle up to any number of bodies as long as they were warm. A never-ending love affair with food (particularly cheese) also gained him the nickname of 'fridge cat.' He could literally hear the opening of the fridge door from a mile away. Living to the grand age of 19, he eventually left us due to a mass that had developed in his abdomen. Because of his age and general health, it was just not operable. Another big personality lost but he left the legacy of a cat's tenacity and how one suffering from FIV has a good a chance at life as a regular puss.

Toots...

This awesome little girl was our 'Rootin' tootin' Toots.' Another puss with a heart condition and an uncertain future. She settled into TC's very quickly and soon had her paws firmly under the table. She made her bed on the kitchen window sill all her own and any cat who tried to steal it, did so at their own peril. Like many females, she was little bothered with the company of other cats but sought out love from mum and dad. Toots particularly enjoyed a brush, any brush. She never got tired of a good old groom. This little darling survived breast cancer twice, so we were absolutely devastated when she developed a rare condition which began to fuse her bones. Although relatively young and seemingly hiding what is a very painful condition, we were left with no option but to help her to The Rainbow Bridge. A greatly missed and fabulous little pussy cat.

Benny...

Once in a while comes along a cat like no other. So singular are they in their behaviour or personality that you wonder if, despite all appearances, it's a cat at all. So was the case with our beautiful big boy Benny. With his rounded ears (tipped due to skin cancer earlier in his life) and his chonky, stocky build, he actually resembled a polar bear from some angles. Ali had originally given him a home after finding out he was diabetic; a condition that only a true animal lover will happily take on. Benny's individuality though, was apparent mostly in his sheer 'uncatness.' He was the direct opposite of the generic feline personality, a creature that is highly strung and ready to bolt at a second's notice. Instead, literally nothing phased Benny. Dogs, people, cars, you name it. Nothing new or strange garnered the least bit of reaction from him. You could pick him up, carry him to wherever you were sitting and plonk him on your lap. Once there, he may or may not have looked around to get his bearings, before falling back to sleep. Benny lived to 16 years old, 8 of those years with diabetes. A growth on his pancreas, which was inoperable because of his diabetes, was the reason he was taken from us. Benny left possibly the biggest hole in our house to date and one which we think will never be filled.

Lily...

This was our beautiful Lily-Pops, a sweet natured girl with a heart condition and just the one stunningly gorgeous amber eye. Part of Ali's original crew, she took to life in the countryside instantly, often gleefully running up and down the yard with her strange little kangaroo jump. She was just a joy to behold. I have made much mention of the never-ending learning curve we are on, and that includes poor Lily's demise. Although our garden lane is very long, over 100 metres in fact,

Lily made her way down to the road and was killed by a car. We were completely devastated and beat ourselves up severely over our lack of foresight. Our property's perimeters, gates and fences have since been fortified. Although not completely 'cat proof,' they do provide a cumbersome deterrent to bypass. This beautiful girl lives on in our hearts and memories.

Humphrey...

Humphrey came to us as an already older gentleman from a fellow rescue. He was never remotely interested in making friends with me. He did, however, form a close-knit bond with Ali that lasted for the rest of his life. Whilst he undoubtedly enjoyed his time here at TC's, he did have his fair share of health problems. Over time, he went fully blind but he adapted quickly, like the complete trooper he was. Eventually, he was taken from us when he developed FIP. His passing left Ali with a broken heart. Humfy's gentle disposition and furry pants are missed even now.

Thomas...

Thomas came to live with us, not because he had any particular medical condition but because he had constantly been overlooked in rescue. Apparently, Thomas was 'too ugly.' Well, their loss was our gain. Sir Thomas Batman Pants, as he came to be known, proved to be one of the friendliest boys we have ever shared our lives with. Whether it be stranger or friend, his genuine affection shone through. He loved his 'lap love' so much, that a growl of protest would be heard if you so much as even tried to move him. Thomas was another baba lost to cancer and we remember this awesome pussy cat with nothing but fondness.

Donut...

Donut is another baba firmly inside one of my mental boxes. He came to us at a very young age; relatively healthy but with some abnormal toes maybe as a result of inbreeding. He was a friendly boy who loved life and, considering my general attitude towards cats, was absolutely no bother at all. His life ended so abruptly and so bizarrely that it left us stunned. Ali, one morning, just cleaning the house, found him dead in the hallway and his wee body was still warm. His true cause of death will never be known but it would almost certainly have been caused by a brain aneurism or an undiagnosed heart condition. We were all robbed of Donut's chance to live and the feeling of injustice still remains; the hurt still so very raw.

Dexter...

Dexter (Big D) ended up with us when his previous family felt they couldn't give him the care and attention he needed. He was an oddball sort of character in many ways. He never bonded with any of the other cats, although was happy in the company of Ali or me. His independent streak was such that, for the first few years with us, he refused to reside in the house at all and instead set up camp in the laundry room. Respecting his wishes, we made it a home from home and kitted it out with beds and electric blankets, even taking him out his meals like the serving staff we are. In his final year, he mellowed and came to live with us in the house. Although still largely ignoring the other cats, he sought out some of the more comfy, warm beds and availed himself of mum and dad's luffs. Another one sadly lost to cancer. Dexter was a special, one-of-a-kind, much missed puss.

Simbaba...

Simbaba was a beautiful big black tomcat who no sooner had been welcomed to TC's when we were forced to tearfully say goodbye. Unknown to us, he was infected with FELV which in no time at all, ripped through his body. We think he was possibly infected when he had a fight with another cat prior to joining us. This is made even more difficult since FELV is one of the nasty diseases targeted by annual inoculations. It is totally avoidable. He was a friendly boy who instantly made friends with the other cats. There is slightly more to his story than I am at liberty to share but suffice to say he was much loved by us and we hope he enjoyed at least a measure of happiness in his time with us.

Mr Tigs...

My abiding memory of Mr Tigs was that he vied with Alfie for the dubious honour of being one of the yappiest cats we have ever shared our home with. He spent his last couple of years with us, after his human mummy died. Being an older boy who had obviously been spoilt rotten, he expected a similar service to resume with us. He was extremely vocal in what he wanted and when. And he usually got it. He was a very gentle-natured boy who fought a lengthy battle with bone marrow cancer. Because his death ended up being such an elongated and protracted affair, he became very special to us and we would put up with all the yapping in the world to have him with us still.

Arthur...

Arthur's story is both remarkable and tragic all at the same time. Somehow, and believe me this is extremely rare, he had survived to the ripe old age of 14/15 as a street cat and was a popular face in his local community. He had a regular food source and some form of shelter and these had almost definitely contributed to his longevity. When a volunteer trapped him and took him to a vet for check-over, it was decided his days on the street were over and he deserved a bit of comfort for his remaining days. So, he came to TC's. In a horrible twist of fate, he instantly became ill and spent the rest of his life, a mere week, in and out of the vets. Despite our absolute best efforts, he deteriorated and we lost him, like so many others, to the dreaded FIP. It was a terrible loss but we did fight for him with everything at our disposal. Although he had been a street cat for so long, he was by no means feral. Our final memories of him are of cuddling a thin but friendly pussy cat, happy in our arms and purring contentedly.

George...

Now this one is extremely tough to write as George has the undefeated title of friendliest cat the world has ever known. Well, I think so anyway. Don't just take my word for it, you could happily ask anyone who ever met him and they would concur. One of his more charming peccadillos was that he enjoyed nothing more than sucking on a man's beard. Odd? Absolutely. But this was just one of the many things that endeared people to him. Whilst I could wax lyrical for an age about George's antics, I would rather that you, dear reader, take note from our experience of swallowing a very bitter pill. Once again, in our never-ending learning curve, we now know to check kidney function of any cat before they go under anaesthetic. In George's case, he was going in for a simple, but necessary, dental. The dental went well, as expected, but he never recovered from the anaesthetic. His damaged kidneys were unable to process properly and he had to be helped over The Rainbow Bridge. It was a horrible, horrible lesson to learn. Numerous factors, diet being one of them, make kidney disease one of the biggest killer diseases in cats. ALWAYS request a kidney function test before an operation. At the time of writing, I think it costs around £40 and is worth every penny. Whether your cat is young or old, PLEASE don't take the risk but learn from our mistake. Gorgeous George, another one-of-a-kind boy and forever irreplaceable.

Bandit...

Once upon a time, it was just Wackadoodle and me. Then along came Bandit. Knowing truly little about cats at the time and having just met Ali, I had my heart set on adding to my small family and was determined to get a sick puss or at least one who had been overlooked in a rescue. Having met Bandit at a local Cats Protection, I passed a home check and got to adopt this awesome little tabby. After some initial reticence from Wackadoodle, they quickly became bosom buddies. This little bundle of fluff became an integral part of my home. He was awesome in every single way; friendly, affectionate, and always in the mood for fun. Further down the line when Ali and her mob joined us, he accepted them all immediately. I think in his little head, he figured it was just more friends to play with. As he started to get older, despite being neutered and happy, he began to wander. At first this was the odd night away. That increased to a few nights away and then weeks at a time. On his return, be it night or day, he would invariably come and say hello, have a bite to eat and fall asleep. In exactly that order. He always looked well fed and healthy and in the spirit of letting him be his own man, we just let him get on with it. Whatever 'it' was. I think maybe the longest he was ever away for was 2 months. Obviously, this was slightly alarming but it was a pattern we had now gotten used to.

Had I known I would never see Bandit again, coming up to 5 years now, I would have grabbed him close, told him how much I loved him and perhaps not let him go out on his last jaunt. But such is life and cats are cats with minds of their own. I can't say he is categorically dead, any more than I can say he's alive. I have chosen, in his case, to take a glass half full approach to his disappearance. Perhaps right now, even as I type this, he is fast asleep in front of a fire, well fed and happy, in a home where he is loved by a family who cherish him. Perhaps he even dreams of the family he used to have, where he had lots of siblings to play with and where he was also cherished and loved. Who knows? Let's hope so.

Mozzie...

Mozzie, Mozzie, Mozzie. He was, without any doubt, one of the strangest little critters I have ever had the pleasure of knowing. So odd was he, that in my mind he barely qualified as a cat. Coming to TC's via a vet who had taken him on but felt couldn't give him the attention needed, Mozzie-man was a 'challenge' from the get-go. As a small kitten, he had caught Meningitis which had left him with quite severe brain damage, near blindness and epilepsy. Complicated doesn't come close to describing our wee werewolf, so-called because he didn't even miaow like a cat but rather had developed this strange little growl like a.... well I actually know what. Under supervision, he liked nothing more than bounding around the garden chasing imaginary 'things'. He wasn't with us long, unfortunately. I think with his health complications, he was never destined to be an old cat and he passed away peacefully one night on Ali's pillow. Ali in particular, took his death extremely hard, having invested a lot of time and love in him; a love that in the end morphed into sadness at a life taken so young. There will never be another Mozzie that's for sure. I just hope that in his brief time here at TC's, with what functioning abilities he did have, he understood he was loved and that he experienced happiness.

Parkie...

Parker (but always called Parkie) is another 'box' cat. He is one of our most recent losses and still too painful to think about. Fellow rescuers asked us to take him in after he had been found living under a car, apparently for some length of time. They figured he deserved a good deal better from the rest of his life. At some point, he had broken one of his rear legs, and because it had been left untreated, it had fused. This left our Parkie with a strange gait, very much like Jake the Peg. As you can see for yourself, he was a very handsome boy and his funny walk just made him all the more adorable. Unsure of how feral, he was we didn't push ourselves on him but left him to find his paws and come round in his own time if he chose to. He spent his early days hidden away somewhere; under beds or behind sofas, only really coming out for food. As his confidence grew and understanding dawned that TC's was a safe place, he really came in to his own. The wonderful boy I choose to remember, is the one who would enter a room with a welcoming chirp that was his way of asking for a brush or for luffs. Parkie's journey with us was a transformative one from a shy, insecure boy to one who developed a lust for life and a friendship to the souls around him. Parkie died after ingesting anti-freeze. Nothing malicious in his death, just a terrible accident but one that led to a no exceptions policy regarding cars on our property. The circumstances of his death were such that I didn't even get to say goodbye to him, leaving me with a heart that is still a long, long way from healing.

***

I was a little concerned, when I thought of including this chapter, that it may be considered a little self-indulgent. After all, we all have furries that have passed and would all love to be able to eulogise them in a public way. If I had my way and it was indeed possible, they would be.

As it is, this isn't a hobby or a passing fancy I have engaged in, it's a way of life. Each of the kids mentioned above, have left their paw prints on our hearts, and helped shape our approach to the care of rest of our family, not to mention the evolution of the rescue itself. Hard lessons have been learned and each pussy cat's story is merely a nod to their memory and the legacy each of them has left us. For that, of course, I cannot apologise.

If I have been a little self-serving, I guess it's because those eulogies that you have just read have been cathartic for me to write. It has been an oddly physical but definitely emotionally draining chapter. I have been able to confront memories, some old friends and some others that are not so old. More importantly, I have been able to take more than just a peek inside some of my hidden away boxes; boxes that I can hopefully fully unpack one day and examine without the associated heartache. I wish the same for you, dear reader.

A chapter concerning 'Gone but not Forgotten' would not be complete without an honourable mention and tip of the hat to my long-serving and trusty friend - my laptop. A faithful computer that I have used for many years. The lappy that helped me write my first book and was instrumental in the near endless nonsense I continue to post on social media. One dark night, in the winter of 2021, a random act of unholy desecration was visited upon it, when it was thoroughly pissed on. With, at the day, no definitive proof, I am almost certain it was Artemis. Although others may have egged him on. Thankfully and fortuitously, the hard drive remained intact and the first half of this book was recoverable. Considering that every single damned penny I make from writing goes in to looking after the kids, this surely shows what complete assholes cats can be.

Toshiba Laptop 2011-2021 R.I.P

Chapter 30 - In Conclusion

Those are some seriously funny looking cats? These beauties are George and Mildred; the turkeys who were saved from the Christmas table a couple of years back. She is a complete sweetheart and he is a grumpy old bastard. I think this picture looks a bit like an indie album cover, I wouldn't listen to the record though, turkeys have dreadful singing voices.

There is a time, about 5 to 10 minutes after all the kids have been fed, when the near silence in our house is only broken by the gentle sounds of lapping as they all clean themselves. These times, when I remember to pause and enjoy them, are some of my happiest. All is well, everyone is replete and peace reigns. It never lasts but it's nice while it does.

Regardless of my numerous moans and groans, I can honestly say if I had my time over, I would do it all again without a thought. It truly is a bittersweet type of life. The lows are awful but the highs far outweigh them. In fact, completely outweigh them. There are no material awards to any of this. The rewards come in the form of a life saved, a happy home given and the enjoyment of looking lovingly at an animal fast asleep without a fear or care in the world. These things bring more happiness and fulfilment than any possessions could possibly match. I think some people do go into the world of rescue seeking some kind of plaudits, and yes, it is an altruistic lifestyle. But these people will inevitably fall by the wayside because 'losing yourself' in the care of your animals often leaves little time for yourself. A day off from the litter trays becomes infinitely preferable to a pat on the head.

I think too, I have learned a lot about myself and I continue to do so to this day. My previous life was vain, shallow, and self-centred and was very much focused on getting the next 'thing' or going to the next event etc. Giving of yourself completely to what, in essence, is all about making another being happy, even to your own detriment, is a life-goal I had never even considered. So many of us work and toil with no clear destination in sight, with only a vague idea of what convention dictates and expects of us. There is a lot to say for the road less travelled, albeit an often smelly and icky one.

I have become a harder person too. Whereas I would have formerly been a people-pleaser, I will now quite happily and firmly put my foot down, especially in relation to our sanctuary. The aforementioned rescue motto of 'you can't save them all' has become a fallback friend and constant source of affirmation in the decisions we have to make. We have been cajoled, browbeaten and at times, downright blackmailed, all in the name of rehoming yet another cat. I used to waver at such times. If someone now threatens to euthanise a cat if we don't take them, I can quite easily dismiss that person entirely. That's on them, not us. Our job is to help cats in need, cats deserving of help, not clean up other people's messes.

I have also learned to say no to my wife, the woman that you have probably sussed, I completely adore. Although happy to admit that she is indeed the boss, I have been able to answer with a resounding 'NO!' in regards to the critters we welcome in to our home. If at least one of us didn't have a foot firmly in reality we would have no end of donkeys, sheep, goats, and God knows what else living with us. Apart from the obvious financial constraints of housing such a menagerie, I have more than an inkling that these animals would find their ways in to our house and end up sharing our bed. I. KID. YOU. NOT.

Spending lots of time with animals also opens you up to their true and often mysterious nature. I'm not talking about the cat who will fixedly gaze at a seemingly blank wall then suddenly bolt from the room in fear, completely freaking you out. I don't believe in ghosts. I do believe though, that cats have a warped sense of humour and do things with the sole intent of freaking us out. I refer instead to the cats that will snuggle up with a sick brother or sister, perhaps some innate behaviour which encourages healing or is just meant as a source of comfort for it. Harrybo, in particular, had an incredibly unique trait. After a final journey to the vets with one of the kids, we would bring the remains back for the others, maybe not to say goodbye, but at least give them a sense of closure for their deceased kin. Having laid the body out in the spare room, Harry would invariably jump on the bed and cuddle the now cold corpse, often spending the whole night with it. The deceased wouldn't spend their last night at TC's alone. I can't even begin to explain what that is all about.

I think it's important to acknowledge too, that although evolution has placed humankind at the top of the food chain, with that position comes responsibility. Whilst most animals are 'subservient' to us, that doesn't give us any licence to use or abuse them. This is a fact that is sadly lost on many. Animals, whatever animal that may be, should be cherished. Only when an animal is viewed as having worth and value equal to that of any other living being, will you truly reap the rewards and benefits that both species can enjoy from forming such a relationship.

It may have come across in my writing that I don't have a lot of time for people, which is largely true. However, an unexpected blessing of entering the rescue world has been meeting numerous like-minded people, people with hearts as big as the moon and many of which I am sure will be life-long friends. Many of these people have become 'Uncles and Aunties' to our kids, caring about them almost as much as we do and spoiling them rotten. The fact they bring Ali the odd bottle of wine and me chocolate makes them all the more special. Incidentally, I'm on a Terry's Chocolate Orange fix at the moment. I'll just leave that there.

If this book has made you think about trying out some form of rescue, despite everything I have said, you were warned! That said, I would of course completely endorse your decision. There simply aren't enough of us doing it. Your life will never be the same again. The daily routines that are necessary for things to run smoothly, make looking forward to the weekend a thing of the past. The days blur into each other as you live your own kind of 'Groundhog Day.' You will be beset by unexpected, often unwanted, trials and tribulations. These need to be met with a type of professional equanimity. However sick, however problematic any one of your furries may become, you will still have others who will need your love and who need their life to continue as normal. You may too, like me, dread the awful pain of them dying. Sometimes I look around my home at a house full of life and in my darker moods see it as merely heart-ache postponed. Of course, this is a maudlin way of looking at things, just as much as it is a faulty type of logic. The happiness you will experience casts into shade the inevitability of death. If ever a saying as apt as 'A life lived in fear is a life half lived' were to be applied, then I am unaware of it.

I honestly thought this last chapter would have more gags in it but if anything, I feel a little melancholic.

I really do hope you have enjoyed the book, whether you

see it as a work of entertainment to be firmly placed in the 'fiction' pile, or, as an old hand at rescue, you have nodded along in agreement thinking of it all as more or less spot on. Of course, there may be certain things I have opined on that you vehemently disagree with, that's fine too. I see life through the lens of a world-weary, middle-aged bloke who doesn't have the time or energy to deal with a moggie's recalcitrant bullshit. I mean, after all, you have to be Pragmatic as a cat man.

Kaylen Fletcher – 27th March 2022

ABOUT THE AUTHOR

Kaylen Fletcher

Kaylen lives in the beautiful countryside of South Down, in the equally beautiful country of Northern Ireland, where he runs his cat sanctuary along with his wife Ali. After a varied career involving mostly retail and social care, he found his true calling in his mid-40's in the world of animal rescue. When he isn't involved in cat care, he is busy raising money for the cats (not that they care) and enjoys gardening, reading, and writing. On his rare days off, he can be found rooting through the book sections of charity shops to add to his already burgeoning 'to be read' pile. A rough estimate is that he will need to live until the age of 421 to read them all. But he feels that nothing is impossible if you have the will and access to a cryogenic chamber.

You can keep up to date with Kaylen and what he's currently working on at: https://www.facebook.com/Kaylen-Fletcher-105612188399664

To follow all the latest shenanigans etc at TC's Forever Home, you can find us here:

https://www.facebook.com/tcsforeverhome

BOOKS BY THIS AUTHOR

Distant Thunder – In The Realms Of Thunder: Part 1

'An unlikely group of misfits and outcasts answer the call to join a venture that will seek out fabled treasures of untold magnitude. A tale steeped in legends of mystery and myth; the only certainty is that the location of this treasure trove is somewhere within the dangerous, mystical Realm of Thunder. With the threat of a looming civil war and a band of companions including an amorous werewolf, a couple of disgraced dwarves and a wizard of uncertain skills, what could possibly go wrong?'

Printed in Great Britain
by Amazon

23528220R10126